D1548809

EDUCATIONAL SYSTEMS FOR
DISRUPTIVE ADOLESCENTS

EDUCATIONAL SYSTEMS FOR DISRUPTIVE ADOLESCENTS

Keith J. Topping

037936

CROOM HELM
London & Canberra

ST. MARTIN'S PRESS
New York

© 1983 Keith J. Topping
Croom Helm Ltd, Provident House, Burrell Row,
Beckenham, Kent BR3 1AT
Croom Helm Australia, PO Box 391,
Manuka, ACT 2603, Australia

British Library Cataloguing in Publication Data

Topping, Keith J.
    Educational systems for disruptive adolescents.
    1. Problem children — Education — Great Britain
    I. Title
    371.93'0941   LC4801

    ISBN 0-7099-2435-6
    ISBN 0-7099-2436-4 Pbk

Library of Congress Cataloging in Publication Data

Topping, Keith J.
    Educational systems for disruptive adolescents.

    Includes bibliographical references and index.
    1. Problem children — Education. 2. Resource programs
(Education). I. Title.
LC4801.T65   1983   371.93   83-9597
ISBN 0-312-23809-6

CONTENTS

PREFACE

Special educational arrangements for disruptive adolescents have mush-roomed over the last decade. In 1975, from concern that this was taking place with negligible reference to the evaluation literature, a survey of practice in the area was undertaken (Topping and Quelch, 1976) and an extensive bibliography of relevant literature was compiled (Topping, 1976). That these papers met a need was indicated by the several hundred subsequent requests for them from various parts of Europe, North America and the Antipodes.

The 1976 survey showed that very few authorities were taking any steps to evaluate their provision, which seemed to be developing in a very *ad hoc* and piecemeal manner. With the advent of the Warnock Report in the UK in 1978 and ensuing legislation, there was clearly likely to be increased pressure to provide coherent and well thought out services, and it was felt that an updated review of the evaluation literature would be of value.

This book draws on the 1976 bibliography, but the material has mostly derived from an extensive computer-assisted search of the literature from 1975 onwards. Data-bases searched were Psychological Abstracts, Educational Resources Information Center (ERIC) and Exceptional Child Education Resources (ECER). A specification of the computer search parameters is available from the author. The last generated by far the greatest number of relevant items. In addition, every Psychological Service in the UK was circulated with a request for evaluations of special provisions in their areas.

Of the items eventually amassed, well over half were rejected. Studies which were considered to have glaring methodological flaws likely to invalidate their conclusions were omitted. Almost all individual case studies were omitted, since it was felt that conclusions drawn from them would be of doubtful generalisability. Studies which were purely or largely descriptive and subjective in nature, and offered little 'hard' evaluation data, were likewise left out. Items which dealt exclusively with children in the 0-11 years age range were usually excluded, although one or two were retained for illustrative purposes. Readers should also note that the chapters on consultation, in-service training, parent training and curriculum include only those items so categorisable that emerged from a search based on provision for disruptive pupils, and are unlikely to constitute full coverage of their individual fields.

The title of the current work indicates that the emphasis has been on the relative effects of different managerial structures of service delivery to disruptive adolescents, rather than being on the theoretical bases, methods and materials in use within particular types of provision. Inevitably, reference will be made to the latter, but only within the organising framework of the former.

Education policy has always been shaped more by politics than by philosophy, and more by philosophy than evaluative evidence. This book at least tries to make the latter more easily available. Nevertheless, although considerable effort has gone into attempting to make it as objective as possible, nothing is ever completely value-free.

The author would be pleased to receive suggestions from readers concerning further evaluation research in this area which should be taken into account in preparing subsequent editions of this book. Research which details hard data concerning academic or behavioural gains is particularly sought after. Given this, reports of small-scale local projects where programme developers have attempted to build-in evaluation would be most welcome. All communications should be routed via the publishers.

ACKNOWLEDGEMENTS

A large debt of gratitude is owed to the staff of the Bibliographic Services section of Calderdale Libraries Department, and to Diana Horner, Susan Barker and Tracy Gallagher, whose helpfulness has far exceeded any reasonable expectations.

INTRODUCTION

Problems of Conceptual Models, Categorisation, Incidence and Causation

This book will not attempt any definition of its subject matter — any specification of exactly what is meant by 'disruptive'. Like 'intelligent', 'disruptive' is a semantically loose, vernacular word, and serves its function best by so remaining, providing this is understood.

The author will take for granted that his readers will analyse what follows from an educational rather than from a medical standpoint. Therefore, there will be little reference to 'maladjustment', a term incapable of agreed definition and heavy with the implication of internal disorder. And if it is pointless to spend pages on categorising the undefinable, there is even less point in debating questions of incidence and causation. It is well known that problems always expand to utilise the resources available to solve them.

As the Warnock Report (1978) points out: 'it is unlikely that early screening procedures will be very effective in identifying the majority of children who may develop problems of adjustment'. Quay (1973) succinctly describes the trend over the last quarter century to eschew the conceptually primitive notion of 'process dysfunctions' existing solely 'within the child'. Most educationalists are now sufficiently professionally confident to be able to take a wider causative perspective; for example, as Warnock (1978) points out: 'the underlying problems may derive from or be influenced by the regime and relationships in schools, and many children may simply be reacting to these'. There is certainly substantial and growing evidence for this point of view (e.g. Rutter *et al.*, 1979).

Spontaneous Remission and Evaluative Criteria

A major problem in the evaluation of provision for disruptive pupils is that a large number stop being disruptive after a while quite irrespective of what has been done to or for them. In other words, the problem behaviour shows 'spontaneous remission'.

There is massive research evidence documenting this phenomenon (e.g. Levitt, 1957, 1963; Eysenck, 1960; Lewis, 1965; McCaffrey and Cumming, 1967; Rachman, 1971; Shepherd *et al.*, 1966, 1971; Glavin, 1968; Clarizio, 1968; Onondaga School Boards, 1964; also see section 3, 'Prognosis' in Topping, 1976). The data of Glavin (1972) are fairly typical – he found that of a large group of children identified as presenting behaviour problems, in only 30 per cent of cases had the problem persisted on follow-up four years later, quite irrespective of any intervention. Lunzer (1960) noted the apparent spontaneous remission of 'maladjusted' pupils who had remained in ordinary schools. A 'persistence rate' of around one-third, and a 'spontaneous remission rate' of about two-thirds, appear with stunning regularity in the research literature.

There are various implications of this finding. One is that the widespread belief that the most effective way of preventing serious problems is by early identification and prevention seems to be something of a non-starter. Another is that notions of 'treatment', especially if directed at within-child 'disease' processes, seem to be nonsensical. (Although medicine, too, has started draining swamps as well as shooting crocodiles – hence Environmental Health.)

A third implication, most crucial for the current task, is that any intervention purporting to ameliorate the disruptiveness of school pupils has to demonstrate a success rate of over 66 per cent before an evaluator would even begin to take it seriously.

Schools may well argue that the stress and disruption for teachers and fellow-students while they hang around waiting for the problem pupil to 'spontaneously remit' is damaging and intolerable. Obviously, one would have every sympathy with this point of view, particularly if one was a parent with a child in a class containing just such a disruptive pupil.

But it is one thing to place a child in a special provision with the objective of thereby changing his behaviour in the long term, and quite another to do it with the objective of enhancing the effectiveness of the educational process for those who are left behind. The two objectives may well be quite divergent, and no attempt to call a dustbin a recycling system is going to fool any evaluator. Thus, a prerequisite for effective evaluation is clear, concise and honest objective-setting by the administrator developing the programme. He who sets too many incompatible objectives for himself doesn't come out of the evaluation very well.

This may also be an appropriate juncture to remind ourselves that children who are disruptive in one situation are not necessarily so in another. The work of Rutter and Graham (1966) and Mitchell and Shepherd (1966) demonstrated quite clearly that while some children are a problem at school and some are a problem at home, there is very little overlap between the groups. Far from expecting disruptive children to be equally disruptive in varying educational settings, it seems more reasonable to expect them to be disruptive only in some lessons, with some teachers, in some situations, in some groups, in some kinds of provision — but not others. Obviously, identifying where the problematic behaviour is arising is the first step towards engineering a resolution of the problem.

Does Anything Work?

Bearing an evaluative criterion of success rates greater than spontaneous remission in mind, evaluations of almost every kind of social or educational intervention have usually proved less than encouraging.

A critical review of research studies aimed at determining the long-term effects of school-related 'treatment' was undertaken by Lewis (1965), who concluded that there was little difference in adulthood between children who applied for treatment and got it, and those who applied for, but did not get, treatment.

Fischer (1978), in a positive orgy of pessimism, reviewed the results of effectiveness research in five areas of professional practice: social work, psychotherapy and counselling, the penal system, psychiatric hospitalisation and education. He commented:

> in all these areas the research indicates that, at best, professionals are operating with little or no empirical evidence validating their efforts, since lack of effectiveness was the rule rather than the exception. In addition, a pattern of deterioration was found in which clients of professionals frequently were found to do less well than people with similar problems who received no professional services whatsoever.

In view of this, there is clearly a great onus of responsibility on programme developers to articulate their objectives, and to do so in a way which renders the achievement or otherwise of these objectives clearly observable and/or measurable. As Lemkau and Pasamanick (1957) point out: 'Any fool can ask a question: the trick is to ask one that can be answered.'

The Paucity of Evaluative Data

Provision for disruptive pupils has been no exception to the bandwagon-growth-unhampered-by-evaluation tendency, in fact it has proved something of a prime example thereof.

In the USA, for instance, Graf (1979) notes that special education programmes for 'socially or emotionally disturbed' pupils increased from 90 in 1948 to 875 in 1966, well before evaluation came into fashion. When Cook *et al.* (1972) essayed an evaluative investigation of 272 of these programmes, they found that only 103 had any data on academic or behavioural gains which might have indicated programme effectiveness, and of these, only 11 had sufficiently clear data to make the results replicable. Very similar problems had been noted by Morse *et al.* (1964). A further difficulty was noted by Sindelar and Deno (1978), namely that the many descriptive studies often had no evaluation, but that the few evaluative studies often were short on description, so the detailed nature of the programme which had produced the effects specified remained something of a mystery.

A similar picture emerges in the UK. Dawson (1980) surveyed a sample of special schools, units and classes for disruptive pupils which had been selected by local education authorities (LEAs) as examples of 'best practice'. Dawson asked his sample what evidence they had of the success of their work, according to *any* criterion of their own choosing. Nearly half could offer nothing at all. Of the rest, many chose 'entering employment' as a criterion, at a time when the odds were very much in their favour. Others chose 'return to ordinary school' as a criterion, and Topping and Quelch (1976) have already alluded to the logical absurdity of removing children from mainstream education if returning them there is the sole objective of so doing.

An Example of Evaluative Effort

Dawson (1980) collected some interesting data from various provisions dealing with disruptive pupils, but unfortunately the results are not presented in a way which allows adequate discrimination (for our purposes) between day and residential special schools, between special schools, units and classes, and between primary, secondary and all-age provisions. This may serve to illustrate the complexities and confusions involved. It is necessary to remember that this is a 'best-practice' (i.e. atypically 'good') sample.

If the criterion for success was taken to be either transfer to ordinary school (whether or not successful), or left at school-leaving age with employment (whether or not successful), or left to attend college or to increase exam passes (whether or not successful), one of these could be met by 62 per cent of the pupils leaving the units during a two-year period. (This is still slightly less than spontaneous remission rate, of course.) Looking at it another way, of the 56 per cent of the children who left the special provision before statutory school-leaving age, 57 per cent transferred to ordinary school. That is, only 32 per cent reintegrated and this is from a survey of primary and all-age as well as secondary provisions, which catered not just for aggressive acting-out children, but also for withdrawn, socially incompetent children, the prognosis for which latter is known to be better (see section 3 of Topping, 1976). The low rate of return to mainstream schooling of various special provisions will be the subject of further analysis later.

However, Dawson comments, 'if success is defined in terms of *containment* of pupils, the schools are undoubtedly successful' (my emphasis). Even here unqualified success cannot be reported, since of the 1,346 children catered for in the surveyed 'best-practice' provision during the two-year period who left before school-leaving age, 113 (or 8½ per cent) were excluded from that provision, i.e. expelled.

Dawson's data also run counter to the aforementioned notion that the younger disruptive pupils are on entering special provision, the sooner they can be 'cured', retrained, reintegrated or whatever. The length of stay in the primary provision was longer than that in the secondary or all-age provision, and the primary special schools had a high rate of sending children on to other special schools.

In all, these recent survey data do not seem particularly heartening.

Behavioural versus Academic Objectives

A problem in the establishment of evaluative criteria is the question of the relative emphasis to be placed on improved behaviour and on improved attainment. Macmillan and Morrison (1979) point out that a reduction in disruptive behaviour tends to become the primary objective for special educational facilities, possibly at the expense of attainment. An interesting parallel in the ordinary school is reported by Rutter *et al.* (1979), who found that in their sample of London secondary schools, the more emphasis there was on pastoral care, the worse was academic attainment.

That this is not entirely an either/or situation is demonstrated by the work of Ayllon and Roberts (1974), who showed that while reducing disruptive behaviour did not necessarily result in academic gains, direct reinforcement of academic behaviours (which were not compatible with disruptive behaviours) did result in the reduction of problematic behaviour. In similar vein, Rutter *et al.* (1979) reported that teachers who taught the whole class rather than individuals, who concentrated on the lesson topic, who sometimes made the class work silently, and who started and finished their lessons on time, enjoyed better behaviour from their pupils than teachers who did not. 'The findings as a whole suggest that children tended to make better progress, both behaviourally and academically, in schools which placed an appropriate emphasis on academic matters.' More specifically, Williams (1961) noted that improved educational attainment correlated particularly positively and significantly with later adjustment in children leaving residential schools for maladjusted children.

It is thus somewhat alarming to find that the curriculum can be extremely limited in all kinds of special provision. Dawson (1980) reports that in his 'best-practice' sample of special *schools* (including primary and all-age schools) 2 per cent taught no art/craft and no physical education, 22 per cent no woodwork or metalwork, 24 per cent no religious or moral education, 34 per cent no domestic subjects and 58 per cent no parentcraft, and only 58 per cent had any specialist provision for remedial teaching in basic skills. (By contrast, the special *units* offered even less remedial provision: 38 per cent.)

When Dawson enquired into the management strategies in use for disruptive pupils within the special provisions, the most frequently cited were: firm, consistent discipline; improvement of self-image through success; individual counselling and discussion; warm, caring attitudes in adult/child relationships; systematic use of incentives/deterrents. This sounds little different from what most ordinary schools would say about themselves (with the possible exception of the last item), raising the question of just how special are the special provisions.

It is interesting that Dawson reports a very marked move away from individual psychotherapy, drug therapy, opportunities for regression, creative art work and group therapy, all techniques regarded as important by the pioneers of residential schools for the 'maladjusted'. Also, while techniques of management derived from learning theory and behaviour therapy are not widely used, they are considered effective by those who do use them, and it is noteworthy that the behaviourally-oriented schools have far more under-age (i.e. under school-leaving age) leavers than schools which are psychodynamically oriented.

It seems fairly clear, then, that schools would do better to concentrate on 'education' than 'therapy', although this does not appear to have been the case with much of the special provision made. As the Warnock Report (1978) puts it: 'special education for maladjusted pupils is not complete unless it affords educational opportunities of a quality which subsequently enables them to profit from further education and training on relatively equal terms with their contemporaries'. Or as Quay (1973) points out, direct teaching is the technique most capable of evaluation — it should be tried first and only discarded if ineffective.

The Concept of a Continuum of Provision

'Maladjustment' was always a rag-bag term, and discrimination between the 'maladjusted' and 'not-maladjusted' always highly arbitrary (Galloway and Goodwin, 1979). It makes no more sense to suppose that children can be neatly divided into the disruptive and non-disruptive, with appropriate educational placement following automatically from the application of the (very sticky) label. As Galloway and Goodwin point out, educational handicap exists in varying degrees in a continuum through the whole population, and there is need for a highly flexible continuum of provision to cope with this.

The Warnock Committee (1978) clearly recognised this, stating 'there will be a need for the increasing development in ordinary schools of special facilities, and of teaching in a variety of ways, to enable as many children as possible who require special educational provision to receive it in ordinary classes'. The Committee went on to recommend that 'some form of resource centre or other supporting base should be established in large schools to promote the effectiveness of special educational provision'.

In many local education authorities it is already the case that a wide variety of provision exists for children with moderate learning difficulties, even where this is not exactly a co-ordinated continuum of resources. Thus 'remedial advisory teachers', 'peripatetic remedial teachers', 'remedial centres', 'remedial classes', 'remedial resource banks' and so forth are quite long-standing features of the educational scene, but a similar range of resources for children presenting behaviour problems is considerably less common.

In the USA, of course, somewhat bolder steps than those incorporated in the 'Warnock' legislation have been taken. As Macmillan and Morrison (1979) summarise it:

> the concerns over labelling, segregation, and the like have been trans-
> lated into legislation in the form of PL 94-142, or The Education for
> all Handicapped Children Act. Among other things, PL 94-142 pro-
> vides for several basic rights: (1) the right to 'due process' — designed
> to protect the individual from erroneous classification, capricious
> labelling, and denial of equal education; (2) placement in an educa-
> tional setting that is the *least restrictive environment* — designed to
> prevent unnecessary segregated education; and (3) individualised
> educational plans — designed to ensure accountability by those
> responsible for the education of the handicapped learner as well as
> to provide an individualised educational program.

Thus to some extent, as Sindelar and Deno (1978) point out: 'concern over the *efficacy* of special class placement, although still an un-
resolved issue, has been eclipsed by emphasis on the reintegration of
exceptional children into regular classrooms'. (My italics.)

A flexible continuum of provision is clearly necessary if children are
to be maintained in the 'least restrictive' educational environment at
any one time. As the North Carolina Department of Instruction (1977)
has it:

> an effective continuum of services is integrated and responsive to the
> needs of individual children. A system is mainstreaming if, and only
> if, there are alternative educational settings available and policies and
> practices function to maintain the child in the least restrictive setting
> for him at the time.

Reinert (1980) describes the concept of a 'Cascade System of Special
Educational Service', which he attributes to Deno, see Figure 1 below.

As the North Carolina State paper points out, 'Support' in Stage 2
could include the provision of a classroom aide, whether paraprofessional or volunteer, or the provision of a time-out or withdrawal room.
Leach and Raybould (1977) note that this stage could include advice
about management techniques, materials and curriculum from a peripatetic (itinerant) specialist, or part-time active teaching by such a
person, as a team teacher in the ordinary class or on a withdrawal
basis.

Stage 3 allows the use of any degree of withdrawal to the resource room for extra help, which then approaches Stage 4, part-time attendance at a special class, which can become full-time if necessary. Leach and Raybould point out that the Cascade misses out an important substep — the move from special class within ordinary school to special unit outside it. After this would come day special school, then residential special school, then hospitalisation.

Figure 1. The Cascade System of Special Educational Service

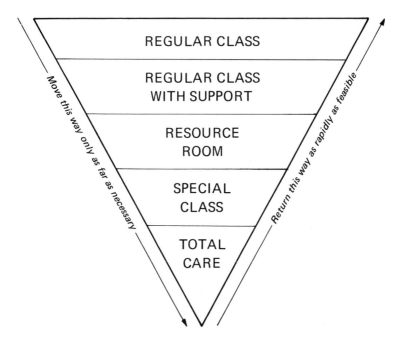

The perceptive reader will by now be aware that the ensuing contents of this book have been arranged according to the Cascade or continuum model — with the most restrictive (and most expensive) resources first, and the least restrictive (and least expensive) towards the end (i.e. the cascade has been inverted).

The North Carolina State paper highlights one further useful point — authorities cannot throw widely varying kinds of pre-existing provision together and call it a Cascade without somebody noticing that what is called a continuum looks more like a lucky dip. A continuum of provision requires purposeful co-ordination and in-built evaluation of the extent to which its objectives are being met.

The Need for Evaluation

The trend towards increasing accountability in education has been accelerated by economic recession. Nevertheless, evaluation still means very different things to different people, and many an 'evaluation' report even today comprises nothing more than vague subjective description or the loosest indications of consumer satisfaction. As Quay (1973) puts it, 'criteria for the evaluation of the effects of remediation are seen to vary in terms of the generality or specificity of outcome and the temporal interval between the remedial effort and the desired effect'. He wrote: 'Improving "social adjustment" or "body image" are not likely to remain in the catalogue of acceptable educational outcomes. Work in the development of short term, specific performance objectives in education is clearly on the rise.'

In 1979 Macmillan and Morrison observed: 'the trend in responsible educational practice is to place confidence in specific interventions that have sound theoretical bases, which have measurable and educationally relevant outcome criteria'. Without evaluation, a great deal of taxpayers' money is likely to be wasted, and a large number of handicapped children further disadvantaged.

Structure of this Book

As will be evident from the Contents pages, an attempt has been made to consider each alternative form of provision roughly in order of restrictiveness and expensiveness, with the programmes which are most costly (per student served) first. In this way the data reviewed on effectiveness can be compared across sections to give some indication of cost-effectiveness.

The sections are further grouped into 'traditional' (in the British sense) provision, provision needing substantial personnel and resources external to the ordinary school, provision needing (rather less) personnel and resources within the ordinary school, provision needing mainly some extra personnel within the ordinary school, and provision needing (rather less) extra personnel external to the ordinary school. Sections on the effectiveness of curriculum change and routine sanctions, both involving very little, if any, extra cost, then follow.

Much of the categorisation involved in organising this mass of data into a manageable form has inevitably been somewhat arbitrary, and it is hoped that the reader does not find this too confusing. Some of the reports reviewed represent attempts to evaluate a complete 'continuum of provision' or 'cascade of services', and it would have been detrimental to have considered these other than in their entirety, which is done in the final section.

The list of references is followed by a supplementary bibliography of items which were reviewed and rejected for one or other of the reasons mentioned in the Preface. They are listed here to save other researchers a long pursuit for limited reward. A third list notes items which looked interesting but could not be located in the UK.

Part One

TRADITIONAL PROVISION

1 RESIDENTIAL SPECIAL SCHOOLS

The evidence available on the effectiveness of residential special schools is very thin.

There have been long-term follow-ups of ex-pupils, often done by or utilising evidence from the headteachers of the schools, using totally subjective and undefined criteria for 'success'. On the other hand, studies which have tried to be a little more 'scientific' have often concentrated entirely on the child's behaviour while in the school, and neglected questions of reintegration and duration or generalisation of any gains made.

Considering the former category first, we can start on an optimistic note with the claims of Shields (1962) that of 216 boys discharged from one such school over an 11-year period, 84 per cent 'made a reasonably normal readjustment to life at home or at work'. Unfortunately the definition of 'reasonably normal readjustment' is less than precise, and it is unclear how the children were rated.

Shaw (1965) kept records of children passing through his special school for intelligent secondary-age boys since 1934. He reported that six had died and six proved uncontactable, but of the rest pronounced 67 per cent 'radically cured', 21 per cent 'improved', 2 per cent 'unchanged' and 10 per cent 'failures'. Burn (1964) reports a similar 66 per cent 'cure' rate at a similar school.

Balbernie (1966) followed up 32 of his ex-pupils between the ages of 17½ and 22. He found five were settled in their own homes, although only three of these were in regular employment. Eight had established 'some degree of adjustment' away from home. Only 41 per cent had achieved any form of stability, and only three seemed really stable. This is, of course, well *below* spontaneous remission rate.

Turning to considerations of within-school changes, Petrie (1962) studied the progress during 18 months in a residential special school of 23 children of both sexes aged 7-12 at the commencement of the study. Few of his sample fell within our terms of reference. However, Petrie recorded that over the 18 months, the children's mean reading and arithmetic quotients increased by statistically significant amounts (although the amount was small, e.g. 92-95, 88-92). While the children appeared to make slightly more than a year's attainment gain in a chronological year, such gains from a very expensive specialist resource still seem unexceptional, especially when compared to the size of gains reported elsewhere (see below). Petrie tried to get some idea of within-school behaviour change by comparing before and after descriptions of the children by one senior member of staff on Bristol Social Adjustment Guides (adjectival rating schedules once widely used with children evincing problematic behaviour). The headteacher's own subjective assessment of improvement was also taken into account. There was some agreement between the two 'measures', and the mean BSAG 'score' improved significantly over the period of study. However, individual children's progress was very inconsistent over time, and those who appeared to progress most in terms of behaviour were not those who progressed most in terms of attainment.

More pessimistic results were reported by Roe (1965) in her study of 72 children aged 5-14 years in eight residential Inner London special schools for 'maladjusted' children (62 per cent of the children were in the secondary age range). While the same unexceptional gain of about one year's attainment per year was shown in tests, the mean Bristol Guide scores did not change significantly over the period of study. Children who originally scored high on the Bristol Guide tended to score lower on reassessment, and vice versa! This latter contrasted sharply with the headteachers' ratings, which suggested that a large majority were perceived as improved.

The major problem with both these studies is that they yield little indication of how the children fared on return to their 'normal' environment. It is well known that even *academic* gains accruing in a 'special', 'remedial' situation tend to disappear rapidly on return to ordinary school, when the 'remediated' child's progress decelerates until his peers catch him up (Chazan, 1967; Carroll, 1972; Moseley, 1975; and Topping, 1977a). And as aforementioned with respect to the studies of Rutter and Graham (1966) and Mitchell and Shepherd (1966), there is no reason to expect children to behave similarly in different environments.

Burland (1979) and Brown (1978) document the effectiveness of behaviour modification techniques in resolving a variety of difficulties presented by junior boys in the context of a residential school, but no published data appear to be available on generalisation to the home environment or on durability of these gains. Cooling (1974) reported on 68 residential schools for 'maladjusted' children, of which 58 catered for secondary-age pupils. He found that of children leaving the schools, 21 per cent transferred to ordinary day school or to a boarding school for ordinary children. The figures of Dawson (1980) from his 'best-practice' sample suggest that around 24 per cent were reintegrated into ordinary school. However, nothing is known of the subsequent behaviour of these children.

The limited data available from the USA, where residential special schools tend to be fewer per head of population than in the UK, are somewhat more impressive. Cohen (1963) cites academic gains of 2.7 years in reading and 2.3 years in maths in a single chronological year. To what extent the elicitation of these gains was purely a result of the teaching methods used, and to what extent it depended on the children's being in a residential environment, is not clear.

Weinstein (1969) reported on Project Re-ed, a *short-term* residential programme for pre-adolescent children 'too disturbed or disturbing to be maintained at home or in a regular school'. The average age on entry was 10 years, so the results are of marginal relevance to our area of interest. Teachers, parents and referring agencies rated the children's behaviour before entry to Re-ed, immediately after discharge and 6 and 18 months after discharge. Immediately after discharge, the percentage of children rated moderately or greatly improved by all sources ranged from 61 per cent to 89 per cent, and this appeared to be fairly well maintained on subsequent follow-ups. As Weinstein says: 'despite the relatively brief average length of stay at Re-ed (6 months), these percentages compare favourably with the two-thirds to three-fourths rated improved in most other studies of effectiveness of treatment programmes'. However, by no means the full sample was followed up – children who lacked one or both parents or who changed parent figures during the study were not included. Further, not all parents fully understood or completed the rating system. At least 8 per cent of the sample were also lost from the ordinary school follow-ups. While these considerations do not render the Re-ed data much less reliable than anything else so far cited in this section, they do reduce the encouragement that could otherwise be drawn from the data.

Data on academic improvement, only available for one of the two Re-ed schools, were 'less striking', and again there was large sample shrinkage. *After* Re-ed, children gained in both reading and maths at about one month of attainment per chronological month. This was about twice as fast as they had previously been progressing in ordinary school. However, Weinstein pointed out that 'learning at the normal rate after Re-ed is only sufficient if the children have completely closed the gap between themselves and their peers' – and this did not occur. It is reported that 'both [Re-ed] schools are currently putting greater emphasis on their academic program'. Weinstein reports that preliminary analyses suggest the improvements at 6 months' follow-up were 'generally being maintained' a further year later. Interestingly, the child-ren's teachers in the ordinary schools after Re-ed tended to rate the children as having progressed behaviourally but not academically, although the tests demonstrated that they were learning faster. This obviously casts doubt on the reliability and validity of either the ratings or the tests, and possibly both.

As Weinstein points out, 'the extent to which the results reflected re-rating effects, improvements related to increased age, or natural varia-tions in behaviour which occur with the passage of time' is not known, and 'conclusions must remain tentative'.

Summary

Within UK residential special schools for disruptive children, the child-ren's behaviour is as likely to stay the same as improve. Academic gains of a year's attainment per chronological year are generally reported, but as the children are retarded on entry they therefore remain so in rela-tion to their peers.

Only one in five children ever returns to ordinary school. It is not known whether any gains within the special school persist when children return to ordinary school.

Completely subjective follow-ups of children who have left such schools have yielded widely differing results on various highly dubious criteria. The mean claimed improvement rate is similar to the spontan-eous remission rate.

There is evidence from the USA that much higher academic gains are possible in such schools, and that short-term residential programmes can be quite as effective as long-term ones.

2 DAY SPECIAL SCHOOLS

In the United States day special schools for disruptive children have not increased in numbers for some years. Jesinkey and Stern (1974) attribute this to the lack of success of such schools in raising the reading attainments of pupils. It is argued that such schools can *control*, but they point out that there are serious questions about the internalisation of that control, and the schools tend to be seen as custodial and segregated. Also, at high school level they have a very big proportion of Blacks and Hispanics on their roll. However, Jesinkey and Stern cite no evidence for these assertions.

In the UK, there is a description of the work of day schools for 'maladjusted' children by a group of headteachers of such schools (Evans *et al.*, 1970), but the only evaluative data of any merit cited are again those of Roe (1965), whose figures they describe as 'encouraging'.

Roe (1965) studied five day special schools in London, which had a smaller proportion of children in the secondary age range than the residential schools referred to in the previous chapter. The results showed that gains in reading and arithmetic in the day schools were worse than in the residential schools, so the pupils in the former became steadily more retarded in relation to their peers. However the day school pupils' improvement in vocabulary was above average, and on a par with pupils in the residential schools.

Critchley (1969) studied two day special schools for children between 6 and 12 years of age (i.e. of marginal relevance to the current enquiry). He found the children's reading and mathematics quotients remained the same over the period of study, rather as Roe had found for her *residential* schools.

Turning to the question of behavioural gains within the school, in Critchley's two schools there was some, though not very great, improvement in Bristol Guide scores over two years, although he too found that the children making behavioural gains were not those making academic gains. Roe (1965), however, found that in her five day schools, the Bristol Guide scores had actually increased! Again, the trend for initial high scorers to drop and initial low scorers to increase was evident, only more so. In the day schools the headteachers continued to rate the large majority of pupils as improved, also.

Simmonds (1965), in one of the schools in Roe's study of which he was headteacher, had Bristol Guides completed at six-monthly intervals for three years on his pupils. Simmonds found a decrease in scores over the whole period, but an increase occurring in many cases after one year, following a frequent abrupt decrease in the first three to six months after admission. Thus, many children got worse before they got better, and it is not clear to what factors this is attributable. Simmonds also noted that withdrawn children responded better than aggressive children in his school (the former group having a better spontaneous remission rate, as aforementioned). In the interpretation of the results cited in both this and the previous section, the age ranges of the schools and the fact that they admitted by no means only disruptive, acting-out pupils, must be taken into account.

Data on rates of reintegration into ordinary school are rather more plentiful than is the case with residential schools. Roe (1965) found that 16 per cent of children from her five day schools reintegrated into ordinary school or further education. Dawson's (1980) figures from his 'best-practice' (all-age) sample suggest that around 30 per cent of pupils reintegrated from day special schools into ordinary school, while a rather smaller proportion (approximately 24 per cent) did so from residential schools. Which is the best approximation to the overall national rate is a matter for speculation. The finding of higher reintegration rates for these day special schools is particularly interesting as Roe (1965) found that the day schools had the children with the most problematic behaviour.

Atkinson (1975) describes the token economy system operated at Highfield day special school for children aged 6-16 years with behaviour problems. Tokens gained for good behaviour and increased work output can be used to 'purchase' extra time at lessons or activities favoured by the pupil, so that the successful child increasingly creates his own curriculum. Fixed break-times are not operated, but the children may use tokens earned to purchase 'free time' at any time during the day. Trips out of school and extra helpings at dinner are also made contingent on token earning. Atkinson states that in the 2½ years of the school's operation from opening, during which the school roll gradually grew to 46 pupils, 16 pupils were successfully reintegrated: 13 into ordinary schools and 3 into employment. A further leaver went to a special school for the partially sighted. It is claimed that only one of these pupils 'failed to maintain themselves' in their subsequent placement. This clearly represents a creditable effort in relation to other data cited in this chapter. However, the token economy system was only introduced after two terms of the school's operation, so these gains cannot be uniformly ascribed to the effectiveness of that particular system. Also, Atkinson does not give data concerning ages of pupils on entry and on discharge, so it is difficult to establish to what extent his figures relate to the adolescent population which is our immediate concern.

In the USA, Budnick and Andreacchi (1967) report very low reintegration rates for such schools, even in the case of younger pupils. However, Marshall (1971) reports on a sample of 60 children aged 6-12 years on admission to a day special school in a London borough. This school did not cater for children beyond the age of 14 years, the result being that 80 per cent of the leavers reintegrated into ordinary school.

Furthermore, Marshall's (1971) study indicated that even with such a high reintegration rate, subsequent adjustment was good, with all but 8 per cent of the children adequate attenders at school, 75 per cent considered to be 'working to capacity' academically, and 90 per cent having no subsequent court appearances. Of the children followed up who had in turn left ordinary school, 75 per cent had had one job for a whole year. Marshall's data are unfortunately clouded by a lack of clarification of methods of data collection, the use of somewhat vague categories, and the use of a possibly biased sample.

Roe's (1965) data on later adjustment at 3-9 month follow-up show that of 24 pupils reintegrated into ordinary schools, 75 per cent had made a 'very good' or 'adequate' adjustment. In this case, however, a very much smaller proportion of the total number of pupils in the school had been reintegrated. Roe does not give any indication of whether academic gains in the special school had generalised to the ordinary school, although presumably in most cases behavioural gains had done. Of the children who left the special schools at school-leaving age to seek employment, 80 per cent were managing to hold down a job. Whether one would necessarily expect children who are/were disruptive at *school* to have difficulty in remaining employed is an open question. Tuckey *et al.* (1973) report that pupils from day residential special schools for 'maladjusted' children more readily acquire jobs than other categories of 'handicapped pupils', 97 per cent of leavers from 68 such schools finding employment at some time after leaving school, but they show a higher employment turnover rate.

There certainly appears to be considerable variety in organisation and methods of operation between different day special schools. One very large authority has even established a day school for 'maladjusted' children catering for children from only one secondary school (personal communication, 1980). Conversely, a neighbouring authority (Waltham

Forest) has a day special school where the children attend only on a part-time basis, to facilitate the establishment of behaviour change in the ordinary school and subsequent total reintegration, and some of the special school staff also operate in the ordinary secondary schools (Smith, 1980; Fry, *et al.*, 1980). It is thus not to be wondered at that the limited evaluation data available are somewhat self-contradictory; however, an attempt at a summary is necessary.

Summary

In day special schools children tend to make fewer academic gains than is the case in residential schools, and become more retarded in relation to their peers.

Within the day schools, behavioural progress is extremely erratic and often not combined with academic progress. The behaviour of many children worsens in the short term, although there may be overall improvement in the long term (three years) in some cases.

The day schools' reintegration rates are very variable, but tend to be better than the residential schools'. Where only 16 per cent are reintegrated, three-quarters of these seem behaviourally well adjusted at follow-up, but where 80 per cent are reintegrated out of administrative necessity, a similar proportion seem behaviourally and academically well adjusted at follow-up.

Subsequent employment prospects for leavers from day special schools are quite good.

Overall, the day schools come out rather worse than the residential schools, unless a high proportion of reintegration is enforced, although they are, of course, less expensive. Day schools are in any case only a feasible proposition in urban authorities where a neighbourhood clientele can be guaranteed.

Part Two

OFF-SITE PHYSICAL AND
PERSONNEL RESOURCES

3 SEPARATE UNITS

Separate off-site units for disruptive pupils are the next oldest established form of provision after the special schools. Such units have existed in New York, for example, since 1940 (Kvaraceus and Ulrich, 1959). The Department of Education and Science (1978b) note that a majority of authorities in the UK now have a unit of some sort. 'The peak year for establishing units was 1974.' Most of these were set up as off-site co-educational establishments serving more than one school. Of the units then known, 25 per cent offered only full-time attendance, 35 per cent offered only part-time attendance, and 40 per cent offered both.

Since 1978, the numbers of off-site units have continued to increase. The ACE Survey (1980) noted the existence of 439 units with places for 6,791 pupils, and only just over half the LEAs responded to their request for data. As ACE points out 'the remarkable efforts of the Inner London Education Authority [ILEA] account for a significant part of this increase – I.L.E.A. now has 226 units offering places to 3,800 students, a total which nearly equals the number of places available in England and Wales as a whole in 1977'.

The ACE Survey points out that disruptive units go under many different names: Tutorial Units, Exclusion Units, Sanctuaries, Adjustment Units, Assessment Units, Withdrawal Units, Support Units, Educational Guidance Centres, Day Units, Nurture Groups, Off-Site Support Centres, Retreat Centres, Havens, Opportunity Groups, etc. They are not solely an urban phenomenon. In 89 per cent of the units students remained on the register of the feeder schools. While this presumably was done to facilitate reintegration at some point to the feeder school, in actual fact the reintegration rate was so low that the effect of this measure was largely to remove any requirement of official recognition of, or accountability for, what actually represented a drastic change in a pupil's circumstances. Few units had managing bodies, and of those that did, none reported the presence of parent representatives. While many LEAs referred to 'consultation' with parents, 'nowhere was there any suggestion that parents or students have the option of refusing referral to a unit'. ACE noted that fewer than one-third of responding LEAs offered an estimate of the per capita cost of education in disruptive units. Of these, the lowest was £60 and the highest

35

£3,500. The average was £1,560 per place per annum.

As Bird *et al.* (1980) comment, the bandwagon growth of disruptive units has given birth to some extraordinary and absurd provisions, like a 'Home Tuition Centre' and a 'Truancy Centre' — from which the pupils hardly ever returned to ordinary schools. Many other commentators have criticised the concept and workings of 'disruptive units'. Francis (1980a) records a member of Her Majesty's Inspectorate outlining the lack of clear definition of what disruptive behaviour actually is, and questioning whether there had in fact been any real increase in the scale of the problem. The HMI continued:

> the worrying impetus given by special units to the generation of yet more demand for their services, and the related fact that their existence often seems to have the effect of absolving schools from the responsibility of examining the relevance and value of what they offer to all their pupils, gives rise to concern about suggesting that units are the solution.

Francis (1980b) lists other causes for concern. Apart from the aforementioned questionable status and lack of accountability of the units, lack of definition of criteria for referral, lack of consideration of parental rights, and marked failure at reintegrating pupils into ordinary schools, anxiety was also occasioned by the restrictedness of the curriculum, the emphasis on 'treatment' rather than education, and the tendency for a disproportionately large number of pupils from ethnic minorities to be sent to the units.

Very similar points had emerged from a massive evaluation research project in Florida five years earlier (Alachua County Schools, 1975). Off-site units were found to have many disadvantages, e.g. the setting was artificial and unnatural, reintegration was very difficult, there were transport problems, the units tended to be used as dumping grounds, 'labelling' resulted in permanent endorsement of children's records, there were no normal peer models and the children modelled on each other's disruptive behaviour (a point also made by Liverpool Education Committee in 1974), liaison with ordinary schools was difficult, and problems of controlling the children were still encountered within the unit.

Francis (1979) notes that many local Community Relations Councils have expressed disquiet about disruptive units, fearing that black children may be disproportionately 'dumped' in them, mirroring the 'ESN' schools controversy in the UK along these lines in the 1960s. Bayliss

(1981) subsequently reported that ILEA had responded to this anxiety by mounting a survey of the ethnic origins of children in units. The report on this survey (ILEA, 1981a) showed there was indeed an excess of pupils of West Indian and African origin in the units compared to the distribution of these ethnic minorities in the adolescent population of Inner London. The West Indian children in the units were expected to number 102, and in fact numbered 177. However, this over-representation was not as great as many commentators had feared.

Much disquiet has been voiced concerning the restricted curriculum in the units. The DES (1978b) noted that while English and maths were taught in almost every unit visited, humanities and science appeared far less frequently, and modern languages, religious education and music were taught in a very small minority. The units were just as weak on practical subjects, with only a half teaching home economics and art, only a fifth offering physical education or games, and only one in ten offering woodwork of any sort. The DES (1978b) further noted: 'Some units lacked specialist resources, particularly text books, reference material and works of fiction.' A few units did have visiting staff to broaden the curriculum. The unit staff's perceptions of their function proved interesting: 16 per cent claimed to concentrate on teaching, 54 per cent on social training, and 30 per cent on both.

Dawson (1980) echoed this finding in his 'best-practice' survey. He found that the units tended to teach fewer subjects than the special schools, with only English, maths and art being widely taught. Rawlinson (1980) notes that in North-east England the units have great difficulties in creating a normal curriculum or a 'normal' school environment. In the USA, Jesinkey and Stern (1974) commented on the units' lack of success even in raising the reading attainments of pupils. Perhaps the most finally crushing comment came from the DES (1980): 'the curricula available in the units are inevitably limited by accommodation and staff expertise . . . taking account of the shortage of skilled teachers in some subjects, and apparent lack of curricular liaison in some instances . . . the whole programme of off-site units for disruptive pupils needs reappraisal.'

However, probably the most alarming feature of off-site units has been the consistently low rates of return to ordinary school. Jesinkey and Stern (1974) comment that while the units may control, there are serious questions about the children's internalisation of that control, and the units tend to be seen as segregated and custodial. Morse *et al.* (1964) in their research analysis of units throughout the USA noted poor liaison with ordinary schools and widespread difficulties with reintegration. In the UK, Liverpool Education Committee (1974) noted that it was easy for secondary schools to see their responsibilities for a child ending with his departure to an off-site unit. Rawlinson (1980) notes that disruptive units in North-east England, whose goal was supposed to be reintegration, had actually reintegrated a negligible number of children. Rogers (1980) documents a similar situation in South-east England, and comments on problems of isolation from mainstream schools and support services. Galloway (1979) commented 'one consistent trend from the available literature is that successful return to school is seldom achieved'. The DES Survey of a year earlier (1978b) reached similar conclusions: 'procedures for returning pupils to school were often less well developed than those for referral to units'. There were 'differences between units and schools about acceptable patterns of work and behaviour', and schools were often unwilling to take back particular pupils, while parents could be reluctant to return their children to schools where failure had already been encountered. Transfer to other schools from the units had the problem of requiring new relationship-building by the pupil and the risk of overloading some schools with a high proportion of difficult pupils. Where part-time attendance at both unit and school was tried to facilitate reintegration, pupils often responded by attending the unit but not the school. Some children had stayed in disruptive units for seven years! However, that this tendency is not inevitable is demonstrated by Mickleburgh (1980), who reported a reintegration rate of 78 per cent associated with a mean length of stay of 33 weeks. Unfortunately for our current purposes, Mickleburgh's unit was for withdrawn as well as acting-out children, and for the age range 5-14 years, so these figures are not directly comparable.

Recent national publicity in the UK suggests that there is concern about the role and functioning of off-site units among the people who staff them. The *Times Educational Supplement* (1982) reports on 'distrust and misunderstanding between schools, units and their clients'. Comment is made on the lack of agreement on the purpose or methods of these 'units', which is particularly ironic at a time of increasing pressure towards the integration into ordinary schools of children with special educational needs. The danger of the off-site 'unit business' becoming so heavily resourced that it becomes petrified and self-protective is highlighted. It is argued that the further development of units would be a blind alley — 'whatever money is spent, there will never be enough units to take out all youngsters who are in trouble at school, and to continue as if this is a possibility may well stop schools from changing as they need to'. Surveys had shown that while large numbers of special unit staff claimed to use various techniques for helping the children in their charge, very few had any formal training in such methods. It had also been found that working in an off-site unit tended to have distinctly deleterious effects on teachers' career prospects.

The criticisms of off-site, separate units have thus been many. Commenting on the situation in the USA, Smith (1973) writes: 'most educators recognise the danger of segregating all "problem children" in one class or school on the basis of a simplistic description. Consequently many administrators avoid developing special class programmes for disruptive pupils.' In the UK, the Warnock Report (1978) cites various disadvantages of separate units, and recommends that 'special units should wherever possible be attached to, and function as part of, ordinary schools rather than be organised separately or attached to another kind of establishment'. Tattum (1982) 'critically analyses the problems and issues involved in the setting-up of special units, which, by its very nature, creates problems of identification, selection, and the reintegration of pupils back into schools'. Having noted that after the 'unit boom' of the early 1970s, the tide of educational opinion is now shifting away from off-site provision, more detached and specific evaluative studies may now be considered more carefully, taking US studies first.

Upshur (DNK) compared the progress of 19 children in off-site special classes ('satellite programme') with 24 'control' disruptive children who remained in ordinary classes. He found that achievement gains and attendance rates were similar for both groups but that the children in the satellite programme had worse self-images than the controls, according to two self-concept scales. The satellite programme operated on a psychodynamic and Rogerian basis, and the children remained in it for five months. In one satellite class the children made an average of 2.4 years reading gain in five months — this class teacher was described as 'preoccupied with scholarship'.

District of Columbia Public Schools (1975) report on a system of off-site units for children excluded from junior high school. These units also had a distinct psychotherapeutic flavour. Objectives for the programme included 70 per cent return to ordinary school within one year, improved self-concept, improved academic attainment for *some*, and others even less well operationally defined. To cloud the issue further, 'evaluation' was undertaken by 'rating' the level of achievement of the objectives: high/above average/average, etc. However, what is clear is that the reintegration objective was not met, and only 33 per cent of the children returned to ordinary school in the period under study.

Richmond (1978) describes Project Advance, a unit-based behaviour modification programme for severely disruptive youth aged 14-20 years. The programme was heavily staffed, with consultants as well as teachers and senior staff. A token economy was operated, children studied pre-vocational and recreational skills as well as more routine academic studies, and a time-out room and unstimulating 'workroom' with strict rules were available. The overall system was very tightly structured and return to ordinary school was achieved via a 'totting-up' system on the token economy and individual contracting. The evaluation showed that children showed no change in academic attainment in reading and maths at all, although their language skills improved somewhat. The parents of the children reported a 60 per cent to 100 per cent improvement in behaviour at home, and only one parent reported no improvement. However, the unreliable nature of parental feedback in such situations has already been the subject of comment in earlier chapters. Behaviourally, the amount of inappropriate behaviour certainly declined – by 77 per cent over a nine-month period. It is not known to what extent this behaviour generalised into an ordinary school situation, or was maintained long term, and no data on reintegration to ordinary school are actually given.

Stein *et al.* (1976) report on a similar programme, which operated on a contingency contracting basis and involved close liaison with the students' families. Attendance was raised to 88 per cent ('normal') levels with a population which included many previous chronic truants. In the first year of operation, no academic gains were evident, but in the second year, an average of two years' gain in reading and maths, and one year's gain in spelling and general information, was recorded. Over the two-year period, 11 out of 44 students returned to ordinary school, i.e. 25 per cent.

Three further studies refer to primary (elementary) aged children, but may prove of interest. Asselstine (1968) described a unit attached to an ordinary school but serving a whole school district. In 12 years of operation, only 28 out of 52 children were reintegrated into ordinary school, and only 9 made any significant academic gains. Asselstine concluded that the era of the special unit was over – in 1968! Allen (1970) describes six similar classes of eight disruptive elementary children, served by a teacher and full-time teacher-aide per class, in a carefully structured and ordered setting. Compared to the control group, the 'experimental' children made significantly greater gains in reading, arithmetic and IQ during the first year of operation. Strangely, no data on behavioural change are cited, nor is reintegration mentioned.

The classic paper in this sphere is clearly that of Quay and Glavin (1970), who established a special class for eight disruptive boys aged 7-10, and studied the effectiveness of this relative to a resource-room programme for such children (see Chapter 8). The class was behaviourally oriented, using reinforcement and time-out. Academic gains were not satisfactory after the first year, and the programme was re-organised to place more stress on academic progress. This proved to be more effective in producing academic gains *and* modifying conduct. However, the special class was found to be costly, unable to serve all the population in need, and tended to result in labelling and transfer of responsibility which made reintegration very difficult. By comparison, the resource-room demonstrated much higher cost-effectiveness.

A more general picture, of provision in one state in the 1960s, is provided by Gloss (1968). Generally, Ohio had espoused the psycho-educational and behaviour modification models rather than anything else, and there was substantial emphasis on structure and organisation. Gloss comments on a 'unit boom' in the 1960s which now appeared to be slackening, with the number of other types of supportive programmes increasing faster than the number of units. This is to some extent confirmed by Hirshoren and Heller (1979), who also point out that off-site units in the USA have existed since 1940. In their nationwide survey, they found that special units were still just about the most frequent form of provision in 27 states, with resource rooms being the most frequent in 22. Reintegration rates cited by special programmes varied wildly, from 0 per cent to 85 per cent.

On the topic of reintegration, the American author White (1979) has some useful comments, based on her survey of the function of specialist teachers of disruptive children in returning them to ordinary classes. Problem areas were: establishing a means of determining readiness for reintegration, clearly defining the procedures for reintegration, clarifying different individuals' responsibilities, establishing guidelines for the selection of re-entry teachers and classrooms, developing strategies to effect the generalisation of academic and behavioural gains to the ordinary school, and finding a means of providing in-service training and support, for specialist teachers as well as ordinary school teachers. It was noted that few specialist teachers of disruptive children had much time allocated for dealing with reintegration issues.

White (1979) refers readers to a review of the 'technology of generalisation' by Stokes and Baer (1977), which describes various strategies under such headings as: sequential modification, introduction to natural maintaining contingencies, training of sufficient exemplars, training in various stimulus conditions, usage of indiscriminate contingencies, programming of common stimuli, ensuring mediation of generalisation, and training for generalisation. Stokes and Baer (1977) reviewed some 270 behaviour change studies and noted how few had programmed for generalisation, despite the obvious requirement that therapeutic behaviour change occur over time, persons and settings to be considered effective. White (1979) comments that the greater the commonality of methods, materials, structures and incentives between special units and ordinary schools, the greater are the chances of generalisation.

Turning now to the limited data on off-site units in the UK, it rapidly becomes obvious that the growth in units in Britain in the mid-1970s was not accompanied by any great increase in care to build in evaluation systems. However, some evidence is available. Mickleburgh (1980) reports on the functioning from 1974-9 of his off-site unit for withdrawn as well as acting-out children of age 5-14 years, with mean age 8½ years. Mean length of stay was 33 weeks, and of 59 children leaving the unit, 46 returned to ordinary school. Of these, 35 were 'not re-referred' to the Psychological Service. Using this latter as a criterion of successful reintegration, about 59 per cent of cases thus proved successful.

McNamara and Moore (1978) report on a primary-age unit, where mean length of stay was one year and mean reading age gain was two years, although the wide variety of tests used for initial assessment casts some doubt on this latter. Of 45 children, 20 were intentionally reintegrated. As in the US studies cited, reintegration rates even for primary age units tend to be disappointing.

Becker (1980) reports on an off-site unit taking largely secondary-age pupils. Attendance rates were good, on a par with national averages. Reading tests carried out on 8 of 23 pupils served by the unit demonstrated a mean 19½-month gain over a four-month period, although to what extent this large increment was due to initial test results being artificially depressed by situational change can only be the subject of speculation. Later results on a different set of eight children showed eight months mean RA gain over another four-month period, which is more in line with the best results reported in other studies. However, of 23 children, only 5 returned to ordinary school, and 3 of these placements proved unsuccessful.

The main source of information on this topic in the UK is undoubtedly the Inner London Education Authority. Roe's (1965) study for ILEA has already been referred to in Chapters 1 and 2. Her comparison of results from residential and day special schools for disruptive pupils with off-site units is coloured by some evidence suggesting that the most disruptive pupils tended to be channelled to the day special schools and the least disruptive to the units. The unit children made reasonable reading achievement gains of around 12 months of reading age in a year, which was more than pupils at day special schools. However, gains in arithmetic were not so good as this, and were on a par in both types of provision. The pupils' vocabulary showed substantial and similar gains in all three types of provision. While the behaviour of the day special school pupils appeared to *deteriorate* (according to teacher ratings), the behaviour of unit pupils, recorded on the same basis, improved. However, this gain refers only to in-unit behaviour, and there are no data on generalisation of gains or reintegration rates.

More recently, documentation on ILEA's aforementioned programme of off-site units has become available via the ILEA Archives Department and the Research and Statistics Division (ILEA, 1978b, 1978c, 1979a, 1979b, 1980a, 1980b, 1981b). Some of these documents refer to detailed costings, which would be of interest to administrators. There is no doubt that the cost is substantial; it appears to be currently running at around £1.6 million. Other suggested and implemented developments have included: increased education welfare support, additional peripatetic remedial teachers, the deploying of psychiatric social workers in schools, on-site units (known as sanctuaries), nurture groups, withdrawal groups and peripatetic support teams in the primary sector, educational guidance centres, additional educational psychologists, 'truancy units', home tuition schemes and so on. No doubt other local education authorities would like to be able to indulge in such a luxuriant diversity of resource provision.

Most of the ILEA documents cited are purely descriptive, although nevertheless very interesting. Two documents are of a more evaluative nature, namely the first and second reports of the 'monitoring and evaluation studies' on the 'support centres programme' (ILEA, 1980a, 1981b). The first of these was intended to be largely descriptive. Not all existent units and programmes are covered by the monitoring study. Off-site centres of various sorts appear to comprise 60 per cent of ILEA's monitored support provision in the secondary sector, with peripatetic support teams comprising 5 per cent. Of all secondary schools, 78 per cent had access to a centre or programme of some kind. The research staff asked about curriculum content. Nine programmes considered this irrelevant. Of the 88 per cent of centres that responded, all offered English and all but one offered maths. A high proportion, compared to the findings of Dawson (1980) and the DES (1978b), offered history and art (83-100 per cent), but provision for games was less good, and offering science or a foreign language also by no means universal (33-82 per cent and 17-30 per cent respectively). Pupil-teacher ratios were minimally 6-8:1. However, attendance rates for off-site centres were poor compared to those of other studies, with mean rates running at around 65 per cent. Reintegration rates for these units were, at around 25 per cent, near the usual low mark, in sharp contrast to the 75 per cent reintegration rate for on-site units.

The second report of the ILEA 'monitoring and evaluation study' (ILEA, 1981b) focused on a 'representative' sample of 32 various on-site and off-site centres. Unfortunately, the small size of this sample makes it likely that firm conclusions about the relative effects of different kinds of service system will not be validly drawable. The 1981b report is particularly interesting because it refers to questions of organisation and management of the centres. There is interesting discussion of conflict between centre staff and their managerial or administrative overseers as to the length of stay in the unit of certain children. There is also reference to 'many limitations' in curricula, although all centres offered English and maths and all but one art and games. Generally, the curriculum breadth reported in the 'representative sample' seems better than that of the fuller sample of 1980a.

So far as reintegration was concerned, five of the nine voluntary agency and intermediate treatment centres in the sample did not expect to return any of their charges to the parent school. The other centres and programmes did aim at reintegration, and in the majority of cases this was a gradual, phased and initially part-time procedure. However, reintegration rates for the sample are not differentiated according to the various types of programme. A large majority of pupils reported liking attending the centres, although many inevitably had some criticisms to make.

A survey was also undertaken of the ordinary schools' perception of the centres. While 20 per cent of the schools had never used the existing facility, the remaining 142 schools had referred 1,900 pupils to centres during one term. Of these, 42 per cent were vaguely positive about the beneficial effects of centre attendance on their pupils. Only 18 per cent of ordinary schools using centres reported that pupils' attendance had subsequently improved, 11 per cent reported improved work and 8 per cent improved behaviour on reintegration. Of ordinary schools using the centres, 40 per cent commented on adverse effects of pupil involvement in such programmes, and there were reports of the behaviour of some pupils having deteriorated subsequent to centre attendance. In all, 26 per cent of user schools complained that centre attendance had had zero or transitory effects on the behaviour of pupils.

Much of this data is now more readily accessible in a book titled *Behaviour Problems in Schools: An Evaluation of Support Centres* by Mortimore and his colleagues (1983). Herein it is stipulated that the main aims of the research were 'the collection of descriptive information' and 'the discovery of opinions about the advantages and disadvantages of the centres'. As the research did not include the provision of hard evaluative data among its objectives, the authors cannot be justifiably criticised for such omissions. The ILEA work is certainly 'illuminative', however.

In addition, information on a sample of 383 pupils was gathered, and it appeared that 42 per cent of these were in centres and schemes primarily owing to failure to attend ordinary school, while 44 per cent had been referred mainly on account of 'disruption' of some sort. Of these latter, relatively few had been referred as a result of threatening or doing violence to teachers or other pupils, and the nature of disruptiveness was somewhat loosely defined, e.g. as 'outrageous', 'rude' or 'silly'. In all, 43 per cent of the pupils were from one-parent families, and their parents were more likely to be manual or unskilled workers than was average for the area, although the unemployment rate among the parents of centre pupils was also higher than average.

Of 162 pupils interviewed, one-half reported that their referral to the centre had been regarded positively by them (if only for its potential escape value), while a fifth had been negative towards the proposal (for fear either of stigmatisation or of the unknown). The remainder were indifferent. The pupils offered few complaints about life *in* the centres.

Mortimore *et al.* (1983) provide an interesting discussion of different management and personal relationship styles found among centre teachers. The centres were asked about their objectives, and all replied that these included the promotion of pupils' learning and the improvement of their general behaviour. However, the former could be construed as somewhat ironic in view of the limitations on curricula in the off-site units, and the latter tended to be construed in tangential terms such as 'improving self-confidence and self-awareness'. There was considerable emphasis on teaching 'social skills', but how this was actually carried out is not elaborated. Few of the centres utilised behavioural techniques. Of the 32 centres, 18 seemed primarily orientated towards 'treatment', 7 primarily towards the acquisition of social skills, and 5 primarily towards the development of academic skills. Paradoxically, when the sample of centre pupils interviewed were asked what they got

out of the centre, by far the most frequent response was 'academic progress' (51 per cent). The centre pupils appeared to attend the centres
more regularly than they had previously attended ordinary school.

A survey of sample centre staff indicated that 50 per cent felt professionally isolated, and 80 per cent viewed their own in-service training
opportunities as inadequate. Teachers in off-site centres tended to feel
that their involvement in such had created problems of career advance-
ment.

It does seem a pity that ILEA's research division has not been allowed
time to address itself more directly to the more crucial evaluative questions, such as: 'do the centres improve behaviour and academic attainments and maintain this improvement on reintegration of the child to
the ordinary school?' Certainly other commentators do not interpret
the ILEA data as favourably as does ILEA itself; hence the DES (1980)
comment that the whole ILEA programme of off-site units 'needs reappraisal'.

Summary

There was a boom in off-site units in the USA in the 1960s which was
echoed in the UK in the 1970s. Separate units are now going out of
favour, however. There is evidence that the units' curricula are usually
very restricted. Some individual units have substantially improved
pupils' reading skills, but others have produced gains no different from
those of disruptive children remaining in ordinary school, and others no
attainment gains at all. Improvement in mathematics is even less frequently reported, and little is known about gains in other curricular
areas. Only two secondary studies report significantly improved behaviour within the unit, and only two report on generalisation of improved
behaviour to the ordinary school. In these cases, the overall success rates
are 50 per cent and 13 per cent, which is less than spontaneous remission rate. Very few children actually return to the ordinary school anyway – reintegration rates are very low almost everywhere. Attendance
rates vary, some being on a par with national ordinary school averages,
some being 'improved' from pupils' previous ordinary school attendance, some being on a par with that of disruptive pupils who remained
in ordinary schools, and some being as low as 65 per cent. Off-site units
tend to have a disproportionately high number of pupils of West Indian
or African extraction. Units operating on a psychodynamic model do
particularly badly, but units operating on a behavioural model tend to

perform only indifferently, despite the fact that behavioural techniques are evidenced as highly effective in many other chapters of this book. Finally, off-site units are very costly, and other forms of provision are more cost-effective.

4 SEPARATE UNITS WITH TRANSITION FACILITY

Some separate units attempt to ameliorate the substantial problems of effecting reintegration by providing for only part-time attendance, with the expectation that the children will continue with some attendance at ordinary school. Dawson (1980) in his survey of 173 'best-practice' provisions, found that 50 per cent were full-time, 17 per cent part-time, 27 per cent full-time *or* part-time, and the rest unclear. However, these units covered primary, secondary and all-age ranges. Dawson found that separate units were more likely to have part-time attendance than 'attached' (to ordinary schools) units, but this finding may have been a reflection of the autonomous units' being more likely to be for the primary age range. Special classes *within* ordinary schools were much more likely to have part-time attendance than units of either type. Of course, to what extent the part-time attendance really formed part of a coherent and detailed strategy of reintegration is not clear. A possible disadvantage of part-time attendance *per se* (i.e. without follow-up) is reported by the Department of Education and Science (1978b): 'It was often found that while the part-time attendance at the unit was good, that at school was poor.'

Once again, it is in the USA that more detailed information on reintegration strategies has been obtained. Cohen *et al.* (1971) reporting on their PICA project, describe how students of 13-15 years receive unit-based instruction in academic and interpersonal subject matter as specified in their Individual Educational Programme each morning, the unit operating on behaviour modification lines. In the afternoon, the students return to their ordinary schools, and PICA staff liaise closely with the ordinary school teachers. Cohen *et al.* report large gains in attainment, improved attendance and substantially reduced delinquency. This is an example of a study lacking description, however, and more detail as to exactly how these gains were achieved would be welcome.

Martin *et al.* (1968) described a unit for students aged 13-18 years, which only operated for the morning session. The reintegration process was broken down into a five-phase system, with clear behavioural objectives for the student in each phase. Martin *et al.* present data for only four students, but this shows the phase system maintaining low levels of disruptive behaviour and high work rates. It was noted that beginning a new phase often resulted in a slight temporary deterioration. Data from phase 5, full reintegration, are less detailed, but at follow-up six weeks after the start of the next academic year, all students were functioning satisfactorily. However, it should be noted that Martin *et al.* only used the phase system with children who expressed interest in it, and therefore presumably had some motivation to return to mainstream.

Masat *et al.* (1980) give a more fully detailed picture of a reintegration system. Within a full-time unit, children being prepared for reintegration move into a special transition class, a privilege which has to be earned. Unfortunately not all students are motivated to return to mainstream. (In the case of 13-14 year-olds, the students may be reintegrated into an ordinary school near the unit as a test run before transfer back to an ordinary school in their home neighbourhood.) In the transition class, materials from the curriculum of the ordinary school to which the student will return are used. A greater emphasis is placed on group work. The student is paced by rehearsal through lessons he will encounter back in the mainstream. He visits the ordinary school several times to familiarise himself with the setting. The child then goes on an initial mainstream contract on a two weeks' trial, starting with just two classes in ordinary school per day, usually one academic and one practical.

As reintegration proceeds, substantial itinerant support is given by the unit to the ordinary school. The 'transition teacher' from the unit is involved in assessing the suitability of ordinary school teachers and classroom situations for the student in question, desensitising the receiving school, closely monitoring student progress, ensuring academic continuity with the unit, supporting the student by counselling or one-to-one tutoring in the ordinary school or back at the unit, providing consultative problem-solving and in-service training services for the ordinary school teachers (largely via applied behavioural analysis: developing programmes, collecting observational data, helping with evaluation, reinforcing the classteacher, etc.), modelling and demonstrating specific techniques to classteachers, aides, paraprofessionals and peers, running group sessions for teachers with similar training needs, providing teachers with resource materials, instigating direct social skills training with the student or peers, holding regular meetings with the student for self-recording and self-evaluation, holding meetings with the headteacher, parents or administrators where necessary to keep things functioning, and so on.

As was the case in the Martin *et al.* study, the mainstreaming contract has specific behavioural objectives — stay on task, complete homework, follow instructions, etc. — and each classteacher has evaluation checklists based on these objectives. The monitoring of the reintegrated pupil is thus very close indeed. However, like Martin *et al.*, Masat *et al.* can only report on the scheme's first year of use with a very small number of students. It is reported that 11 students have reintegrated satisfactorily, but it is not known if any failed, and if so how many and why. Masat *et al.* comment that the children in transition often behaved well in the time spent in ordinary school and reserved acting out for the time spent back at the unit. Staff in ordinary schools were initially very apprehensive and resistant to the reintegration, but this resolved when they found that the reintegrated adolescents often behaved better than many 'normal' students.

Summary

There is evidence from the USA that part-time attendance at separate units can produce academic gains as great as full-time attendance. Detailed, tightly organised and behaviourally specific phased reintegration strategies have shown success in maintaining improved behaviour back in the ordinary school, but substantial support from the unit for the ordinary school seems necessary to achieve this. There is little evidence of success in this field in the UK (but see Chapter 22).

The amount of planning and effort involved in reintegrating students from separate units would seem to call into question the desirability of removing them from the ordinary school in the first place.

5 'ALTERNATIVE' SCHOOLS

There is a certain amount of philosophical literature on this subject, a small amount of descriptive literature, and virtually no evaluation. To some extent this is doubtless because the objectives of such organisations tend to be couched in very vague terms which refer more to what they are not than what they are, and also because the provisions themselves open, change and close at sometimes bewildering speed.

Some of the 'Reporting Centres' or 'Suspension Centres' set up by some authorities have assumed the mantle of 'alternative schools' or 'street academies', but usually briefly. Likewise, there have been some projects in urban areas linking Social Services department provision, often under the auspices of 'intermediate treatment' funding, with some kind of Education Department input for 'disaffected' 15 and 16 year-olds. No evaluative data for such programmes have come to light, however.

Some data are available from the US. Olsen (1974) described several alternative schools, a few of which reported gains in achievement test scores, lower rates of truancy and discipline problems, and improvement in student attitudes, but much of the data was highly subjective in nature. The Los Angeles Alternative School found no changes in the achievement test scores of its students above or below the level expected on the basis of prior school performance (Nelson and Kauffman, 1977).

Nor is there much evidence that participation in work-study and work-experience programmes by way of an alternative to ordinary schooling is particularly successful. Both Ahlstrom and Havighurst (1971) and Jeffrey and Jeffrey (1969) report very limited positive outcomes from such schemes (although as was noted in Chapter 2, 'disruptive' children do fairly well when they enter the real job market).

A particularly interesting programme at 'Commando Academy' is described by De Roche and Modlinski (1977). This is an alternative school staffed primarily by black ex-criminals, which features tight discipline, teaching in vocational and self-help skills, and paid work experience. Children aged 13-17 years are referred there by the courts. The attendance rate is said to be 72 per cent, but no other even quasi-evaluative data are offered.

Summary

There is negligible evidence that 'alternative' schools are effective, and
indeed many are not capable of evaluation.

6 SUSPENSION CENTRES

Grave disquiet exists about the desirability and effectiveness of the practice of 'suspending' pupils. Garibaldi (1979) comments:

> Recent reports and research studies have reminded the public of the abuses and excesses of suspensions; that more black students than white students are suspended; that suspension for truancy and class cutting in fact 'rewards' students with the very release from school they are seeking; and that suspended students often are those who can least afford to miss academic instruction. Further, suspension not only harms students, it also harms communities where students may loiter before returning home.

In the USA, there is the additional consideration that suspending pupils immediately reduces the school's funding, which is based on average daily attendance.

Nevertheless, the use of suspension has been extremely high in the USA. Williams (1979) reports that in a 1972-3 survey of 2,862 schools enrolling over 24 million students, over one million students were suspended at least once during the school year. At the secondary level, one in every 13 students experienced suspension.

It is doubtful whether suspension rates reach this level anywhere in the UK. York *et al.* (1972) report that in the two academic years 1967-9 in Edinburgh, 31 children were suspended. However, Birmingham Education Committee reported in 1976 that three units catering for 30-40 suspended children a year dealt with 'a minority of those suspended' in the city. Galloway (1981) reports 266 pupils were suspended *for longer than three weeks* in Sheffield in 1975-9. Bayliss (1982) reports increases in the number of suspensions in Manchester secondary schools from 223 in 1980-1 to 282 in 1981-2. The rise was largely due to an increase in the use of suspension with children who had assaulted other children or damaged buildings. There was no increase in the use of suspension with children who had actually assaulted teachers, although suspension was tending to be used more with children who had threatened this. The proportion of prolonged suspensions lasting longer than 80 days remained roughly the same, being 32 in number, but there were a small number of cases of 'extremely long duration'.

There is, however, no doubt that the suspension rates vary greatly from area to area and from school to school in a way which appears to have little to do with the incidence of disruptive behaviour, if this latter is viewed at all objectively. York *et al.* (1972) reported that of 41 suspensions in Edinburgh, 30 per cent were of primary-aged children, the majority of whom were excluded from special schools. This made the rate of exclusion from special schools 30 times the rate of exclusion from ordinary schools. York *et al.* also found that twice as many children were suspended during the winter as during the summer, and that suspensions tended to peak in the middle of the term. Galloway (1981) supports this, reporting peaking suspension rates in November and again in February/March. Grunsell (1979) cites evidence of unrecorded suspensions and of markedly different rates of suspension from school to school, with a significant over-representation of the West Indian community amongst the permanent suspensions. Galloway (1976) found that comprehensive schools newly constituted from old selective schools were more prone to exclude children, while Longworth-Dames (1977) found that this difference did not continue to exist in an area which had reorganised some time previously. In the USA Williams (1979) reports an analysis of suspensions in four schools, showing that in three schools attendance violations constituted the most frequently cited category of behaviour leading to suspension (35-45 per cent), while it accounted for only 10 per cent in another. Likewise suspension for fighting varied from 10 per cent to 30 per cent between different schools. Galloway (1981) concludes:

> schools varied widely in the number of pupils they excluded and the differences were consistent from year to year. Exclusion was *not* strongly associated with socio-economic disadvantage in the school's catchment area. Schools which excluded a lot also referred many pupils for special education. Exclusion rates reflected each school's own idiosyncratic policy or practice.

It seems well accepted that the purpose of suspension is not to help the suspended pupil. York *et al.* (1972) note that of the suspended children they followed up one to three years later, only 16 per cent were at home and attending ordinary school. The rest were in care, residential schools or psychiatric hospitals. Fiske (1977) documents a strong trend to find alternatives to suspension in the USA, and notes that the disadvantages of suspension are not only to the student, but also to the school, which gets involved in a mass of time-consuming administrative procedures as well as (in the USA) losing funding.

Williams (1979) and Garibaldi (1979) list a wide range of such alternatives. Garibaldi points out that the mode of operation of these shows prodigious variety in different schools. Some had no set time limits, and students would be placed in the 'suspension alternative' for periods varying from 40 minutes to a whole term. Most programmes were not clearly defined in terms of the delivery of services. Some were academically oriented, some counselling oriented, while some seemed to provide neither. In some cases there was no theoretical, let alone empirical, model for the intervention, which rested solely on the 'charisma' of the programme director.

Provisions in this area also vary widely in their degree of integration with the ordinary school system. Some are completely isolated units, as described by the Birmingham Education Committee (1976). In this case reintegration rates are reported to be very low, with only four of the approximately 70 children dealt with over two years returning to ordinary school. Swailes (1979) describes a suspension centre in a fairly rural area in Northumberland, to which some children travelled 25 miles each day. The centre has no structured academic programme. Length of stay ranges from 8 to 28 weeks with a mean of 15 weeks. Although the centre only admits suspended children who are 'very likely to be able to reintegrate to ordinary school', less than half the pupils actually are reintegrated. Smith (1973) describes a day 'school' for suspended pupils in the USA which boasted excellent physical facilities. The children stay for between one month and one year, and attendance rates are said to be 75-80 per cent. Fifty-four out of 100 students were reintegrated during the year in question.

A different system altogether, but also very isolated from the mainstream, is that described by Leeds City Council (1975), who established 'Reporting Centres' for suspended pupils. The pupils would report in the morning to collect their assigned work for the day, complete the work at home, and report back with the finished assignment in the late afternoon. No evaluative data are available for this system, however.

Haussmann (1979) describes a somewhat less isolated system, a suspension unit serving a complex of several schools. Classroom assignments are sent by the ordinary schools to the unit. No evaluative data are cited, although the advantages of the students' keeping up with current classwork and being kept off the streets at less risk of delinquent involvement are mentioned. This particular system has strong legalistic and punitive overtones. The unit was seen by the courts as a method of disposal which stopped short of incarceration. Students could earn 'early release' by good behaviour, while violation of the unit rules just resulted in a longer stay. The units were said to have a 'structured, quiet atmosphere' wherein violence was 'isolated and restrained'. Despite the absence of evaluative data, there were plans to extend the scheme to provide three more school complexes with units.

The role of suspension 'centres' within ordinary schools is described by Garibaldi (1979). In the USA, these are typically well staffed, much academic work is set by the usual subject teachers, and considerable time is devoted to group or individual counselling. Most centres limit their students' contact with their regular classmates, although this isolation can serve a positive or negative function.

Sweeney-Rader *et al.* (1980) describe such a unit in one high school of 4,600 students aged 15-18 years. Previously, UK-style suspensions of 1-5 days with mandatory reinstatement had been found to be ineffective. The unit was able to retain students longer and supervise them intensively, preventing misconduct in school or the neighbourhood. However, time spent in the unit still did not exceed five days, and averaged three. Much of the day was devoted to group counselling. On discharge, the unit continued to monitor the students' progress, although little support was offered to the ordinary school system. Of 123 students catered for in one year, 53 per cent decreased their absenteeism, 62 per cent were not re-referred for suspension, and 36 per cent showed a decrease in the number of incidents involving a need for discipline. This does not compare terribly favourably with spontaneous remission rates.

Nelson (1979) reports on three years' use of an in-school suspension centre where good attendance and academic work were stressed. He reports much improved attendance rates (to 94 per cent), a drastic reduction in the number of home suspensions, much reduced vandalism and a much reduced incidence of fights, racial tension and use of tobacco and drugs. With respect to these claims, it should be mentioned that the school was in a fairly dire state before the establishment of the centre.

Summary

A school's suspension rate tells you as much about the school as it does about the pupils. Suspension seems to serve only to give the rejecting school a brief respite — there is no evidence that it produces improved behaviour in the student. It does nothing to help the suspended pupil, and may well be damaging.

A wide range of types of 'suspension unit' have existed, both in and out of ordinary school.

Out-of-school suspension units tend to increase greatly the time suspended pupils spend out of mainstream education, and reintegration rates are very low.

In-school suspension centres with delimited duration of stay (e.g. maximum of five days) show better results than merely debarring children from school, but even here the results tend to be no better, or somewhat worse than, spontaneous remission.

Part Three

IN-SCHOOL PHYSICAL AND PERSONNEL RESOURCES

7 SPECIAL CLASSES

In this section special classes (or 'units') situated within an ordinary school will be considered. These seem to be generally more acceptable in philosophical terms than off-site separate units; for example the Warnock Report (1978) states: 'we recommend that special classes and units should wherever possible be attached to, and function as part of, ordinary schools, rather than be organised separately or attached to another kind of establishment'. Schultz *et al.* (1971), in their survey of provision in the USA, noted that special classes were the most prevalent kind of programme offered to disruptive children. The within-school special class has, of course, been a feature of the integration-oriented Scandinavian special education system for some time (e.g. Chazan, 1973).

Nevertheless, enthusiasm for this type of resource has been by no means general in the UK. The DES (1978a) reported: 'For most heads, the keys to sound discipline were a challenging curriculum and good personal relationships between teachers and pupils. Every teacher must bear an equal responsibility. Perhaps for this reason, one or two schools, when offered a behavioural unit by the L.E.A. preferred to use the resources in a more general way.' Foulkes (1980) reports some similar feeling in the North-east of England. Galloway *et al.* (1978) report on some Sheffield headteachers' arguments against special classes, viz.

> 1. placing difficult children together encourages them to learn deviant behaviour from each other, 2. a separate group is an anomaly in a comprehensive school, for the same reasons that special schools are seen as anomalous in a non-selective education system, 3. the groups can lead to an unhealthy division between pastoral care staff and subject teachers.

Such classes certainly have operational difficulties. There is frequent comment on the 'isolation and uncertainty' felt by teachers of such classes (DES, 1972; Bartlett, 1970). The wide range of age and ability makes effective teaching very difficult (Bartlett, 1970). The class may be used as a dumping ground (Bartlett, 1970; Alachua County Schools, 1975), the setting is unnatural, there are no 'normal' peer models, 'labelling' occurs which will stick on the child's record, and reintegration can

61

prove very difficult (Alachua County Schools, 1975). The DES (1972) sounded various other warnings in their report of their inspection:

> The cocooning effect of a warm secure special class was sometimes observed to foster dependence and immaturity. In a number of instances so tolerant was the régime that the pupils did virtually what they liked; relief from strain is in itself insufficient unless something positive is offered in its place. In a few classes practically no demands were made on the children: they were over-indulged in a régime which encouraged immature behaviour. The absence of expert teaching was so conspicuous in some classes that it would be difficult to substantiate their claim to be 'special' in any except a derogatory sense.

The majority of children enjoyed coming to the classes reported on by the DES (1972), but the report concludes:

> unless pupils in the special class are able to play a reasonable part in the social and intellectual life of the school as a whole, a special class may well be productive of its own kind of segregation and deprivation. 'Integration' does not occur spontaneously. It requires careful planning and constant vigilance, as well as effort, sympathy, understanding and some degree of imagination not only on the part of the special class teacher but of the school as a whole, particularly of the head.

In the USA, Graf (1979) found that in her study of 39 special classes, 11 of which were at high schools, similar criticisms applied. (It should be noted that the study took place in the classes' first year of operation.) Classroom observations showed that the teachers spent only 25 per cent of their time teaching. 'These teachers generally were unable to cope successfully with the behavioural deviations of their students [and] spent a disproportionate amount of their time in conflict situations.' According to PL 94-142, each child was supposed to be following an Individual Educational Programme (IEP), but Graf found that these often consisted of long-term aims but no short-term objectives. Many IEPs were missing or incomplete, and of the few that were complete many had been filled out *post hoc*. There was no specific curriculum, and what *was* taught reflected the teacher's own orientation rather than the students' needs.

In the classes, 27 per cent of the teachers complained that both they and their students were isolated. There was a lack of definition of the task in hand and a lack of in-service training. The heads of the schools in which the classes were situated correspondingly complained of the special class teachers' inexperience, and many heads saw the classes as a complicating disruption to the organisation of the school. Administrators of the programme exhibited great variability in the goals they cited for it. Thirteen administrative officers named eight different goals − the only common one being to 'provide structure and curtail acting-out'.

Nevertheless, the teachers, administrators and parents rated the programme a success although what was said in interviews was often much more pessimistic than what was written on questionnaires. In fact, parental liaison with the special classes was very poor, and it was clear that the parents equated success of the programme with 'relief and gratitude that they were no longer being harassed by school authorities about their child's deviant behaviour'. (A similar finding is reported by McKinnon, 1970.) The parents wanted the children to stay in the special classes and not return to mainstream. There was no definition of what the criteria for suitability for return to mainstream were. In the first year of operation, 17 per cent of children were intentionally reintegrated. Graf points out that the goals of teachers, headteachers, parents and administrators for the programme were quite different. This naturally renders evaluation somewhat difficult. It also renders the probability of programme success very small. Graf concludes 'this program was hastily conceived, poorly designed and badly executed'.

A number of evaluative studies of special class placement exist, but the majority are concerned with the primary (or 'elementary') age range. It may nevertheless be of use briefly to consider these.

A comparison of the effectiveness of a very structured and delimited special class placement with a permissive, child-centred regime and with regular class placement is reported in Phillips and Haring (1959) and Haring and Phillips (1962). The structured class students made about two years' progress in reading, language and arithmetic in one year while the two other groups made one year's progress. The 'structured' group also made substantially greater behavioural gains, which generalised to some extent to the home. However, there are doubts about the comparability of the 'control' groups, class size is not well controlled for, and there are no long-term follow-up data to indicate if these gains lasted. Haring and Whelan (1965) re-reported these data and the further development of their theories in a later paper.

Rubin *et al.* (1966) found no significant differences between their control and experimental groups on a variety of measures, although there was a trend to improved behaviour inside the class but not outside of it. They noted, however, that what went on in the special class was little different from what occurred in the regular class, and the fact that the former was considerably smaller still did not mean that children actually experienced more contact time with the teacher.

Reports of the Santa Monica Project are found in Hewett (1968) and Hewett *et al.* (1969). A complex multi-cell experimental design was used with six classrooms of nine children aged 8-12 years, to determine whether a token-economy 'engineered' classroom would improve student task attention and academic achievement. Results showed the 'engineered' class to do better than controls on attention to task and arithmetic gains, but not on reading gains. There was improvement in behaviour within the special class. However, there are doubts about the extent to which all the students qualified for the 'e.d.' label. Also, improvement of apparent task attention as a goal in itself seems pointless unless it results in improved attainment or behaviour. Further, one of the classes showed improved task attention when it switched from experimental to control condition, suggesting a 'novelty' effect might have been operating in the experimental design.

Glavin *et al.* (1971a) reported on two years' usage of special classes with 'conduct problem children' of average age 9 years. In the first year, the programme emphasised the elimination of deviant behaviours and the acquisition of attending behaviours as precursors for academic gain. Programme emphasis was changed in the second year to stress rewards for academic performance within the context of a highly structured classroom programme. The first year showed very small academic gains but the second year showed much improved behaviour and academic gains of two years' progress within the twelve-month period.

In the UK, Chalk (1975) describes 'Sanctuary Units' in primary schools, but classteachers' behaviour ratings of children who had had this service showed no significant improvement. In this context, it is worth mentioning the 'nurture' groups operating at the primary level in London (see Ingram, 1972; Boxall, 1973) but no evaluation seems to be available.

Considerably fewer detailed studies of special class effectiveness are available at secondary level. Filipczak *et al.* (1979) report on such classes operating in rural, urban and suburban areas in the very substantial seven-year PREP project. Within the special classes, students received intensive daily basic skills instruction and social skills training, and 'contingency management procedures of varying complexity were used'. Students spent part of each day in regular school classes. PREP students showed academic gains of 1½ to 2 years' progress in a year, substantially better than control groups wholly in regular classes or solely exposed to 'social' training. At follow-up two years later, however, the gains of the experimental group had dissipated and they were now at the same level as the controls. (Note: 67-80 per cent of the samples were lost at follow-up.) Data on behavioural gains did not prove to be reliably gatherable.

Walker *et al.* (1969) studied the on-task behaviour of 10- to 12-year-old acting-out children in special classes of six pupils. Programmed instruction and a token economy were employed. Baseline on-task time was 39 per cent and this rose to 90 per cent in the special class. Three months after return to ordinary class, on-task rates were 72 per cent. However, this does not represent a very long-term follow-up, and as previously cited studies show, high on-task rates do not necessarily result in increased attainment or improved behaviour.

A similar study was reported by Broden *et al.* (1970a) with disruptive 13- and 14-year-olds. Baseline study behaviour was 29 per cent, rising to 57 per cent when social approval was made contingent, and to 74 per cent when a token economy was instituted. At this stage, the improvement was not generalising outside the token system, so a response cost system was operated for the rest of the day, when study behaviour increased to 80 per cent throughout. A reversal condition demonstrated deterioration.

The classic long-term studies in the field are those of Vacc (1968, 1972) although his subjects were only on the fringe of secondary age, being of average age 10½ years on entry to the special class. He found (Vacc, 1968) that the special class children achieved better on attainment tests than control children in ordinary classes, and that the special class children improved on a behaviour rating while the regular class children deteriorated in this respect. A very long-term follow-up was carried out nearly six years from the date of entry to the special class (Vacc, 1972), which showed that the effects of the special class had all dissipated, and these children were now at the same level as the controls on measures of attainment, behaviour and sociometric status. Vacc concluded 'if special classes have any advantages over regular classes for emotionally disturbed children, it exists only as long as the children remain in the special program'.

In the UK, Galloway (1980, 1981, 1982) studied seven Sheffield secondary schools with special groups for disruptive pupils, and three without such groups. The schools with special classes varied greatly in size, catchment and policy — they by no means faced similar problems. Some groups had a therapeutic orientation, others a punitive one.

The groups were all full time and all had a very favourable staffing ratio (much higher than that in special schools), with very experienced teachers. The average length of stay varied widely, from 3-19 weeks. Ordinary subject teachers rarely provided work for pupils in the groups, even where sought, and this resulted in a restricted curriculum and re-integration problems. The existence of the groups had not made any difference to the numbers of pupils suspended, excluded or referred for special school placement, nor had they made any difference to the amount of corporal punishment used in the schools. However, the children in the classes showed a high rate of on-task behaviour (70 per cent). The proportion of teachers in the host schools who felt the children in the special classes might benefit from the experience varied from 21 per cent to 92 per cent between schools. The latter figure occurred in a school where the stay in the special class was very short and return to ordinary classes very speedy. Galloway (1981) concludes: 'Special groups can complement an effective discipline and pastoral care system, but cannot create one.'

In theory, special classes within ordinary schools should presumably find reintegration easier than would be the case with off-site units. This is not necessarily so in practice, however. Schultz *et al.* (1971) note enormous variation in the percentage of children returning to ordinary education from special programmes: from 5 per cent to 90 per cent. Great Falls Public Schools (1971) report only a 50 per cent reintegration rate from special classes for 6- to 14-year-old children whose over-riding goal is reintegration. Deem and Porter (1965) report a similar finding, adding dryly that 'teachers expressed a need for more time, not more pupils'. Callely and Rees (1980) describe an attempt to facilitate re-integration by maintaining all special class children on a partial ordinary class timetable, and Foulkes (1980) reports impressionistically that this technique, together with the formulation of clearer aims and objectives and establishing contracts between pupils and school, has resulted in a faster turnover of children.

Summary

The advantages and disadvantages of special classes are considered. Aims and objectives for such classes may be unclear or conflicting, and day-to-day practice may not correspond with policy statements.

There is evidence from the USA that special classes for primary-aged children can show very substantial academic gains (two years' attainment in one year) and behavioural improvement where the class is highly structured and academic work strongly emphasised. Otherwise, results are disappointing even in the short term.

At secondary level, there is evidence from the USA that part-time special classes can produce substantial academic gains (1½ to 2 years per year) and that full-time classes can produce both behavioural and academic gains, but in both cases these gains had disappeared at long-term follow-up. However, there is evidence that carefully designed token economies can produce medium-term post-programme improvements and be generalised to other situations.

In the UK, the existence of special classes has not reduced the number of suspensions, exclusions or referrals for special education. Many special classes still find reintegrating children very difficult, although part-time attendance throughout may facilitate this.

8 RESOURCE ROOMS

The concept of a resource room as a 'less restrictive' alternative to the special class is described (variously) in Leach and Raybould (1977), Hamill and Wiederholt (1972), Reger and Koppman (1971), and by numerous other authors listed in Sindelar and Deno (1978). Part-time withdrawal from some lessons has been a very common procedure in UK secondary schools for children with learning difficulties, particularly in reading, but rarely has this model been applied to disruptive children.

As Leach and Raybould (1977) point out, the resource room can offer a great deal more than teaching time. The resource-room teacher can (1) consult with a child's regular teachers; (2) assist with academic or behavioural assessment and programming *in situ*; (3) provide appropriate materials and resources; and (4) tutor individuals within the regular class, as well as offering any combination of these with any amount of withdrawal teaching. All this could take a great deal of time, of course, not to say prodigious expertise and diplomacy.

An interesting example is described by Morgan (1980) and Rideout (1980), who note that disruptive children are rarely disruptive in all lessons. After referral and full conferencing, a child might be admitted to the 'Support Class' for the greater part of the school day, where he/she carries out formal work and is debarred from mid-session breaks. In the ensuing few weeks, break time and attendance at ordinary classes is steadily increased. Six different (mostly senior) staff members teach in the support class at various times of the week, although much of the formal work done is set by the child's ordinary subject teacher. The boundary between the support class and the ordinary classes is kept as open and flexible as possible, and the involvement of several members of staff further serves to reduce isolation. The average length of stay in the unit is four weeks.

The need for resource rooms to offer great flexibility and wide variety in scheduling, but combined with clear and firm structure, is also noted by Alachua County Schools (1975), where it is also emphasised that the room and its teacher is a resource to the ordinary teacher as well as the student. The resource room has the advantage of being an immediately available in-school resource, of serving a greater number of children than would a special class, of having much reduced problems of reintegration, and of offering support for the ordinary classteacher. However, there may be difficulties with timetabling and organising work programmes, and 'dumping' can still occur if not guarded against.

Sindelar and Deno (1978) review the results of 17 studies of resource-room programming which included relevant comparison groups. They concluded that academic gains from such provisions were not uncommon, but that behavioural gains had not been established. Nevertheless, the most carefully designed studies supported the effectiveness of resource programming. Unfortunately for our purposes, few of the studies considered such provision for disruptive adolescent pupils, and even fewer reported on long-term follow-up.

The only substantial work in the field comes from the reports of Quay and Glavin (1970), Glavin *et al.* (1971b), Quay *et al.* (1972), Glavin (1973) and Glavin (1974), who describe the evaluation of a two-year resource-room programme and one- and two-year post-programme follow-ups. Over two consecutive years these workers studied groups of 27 and then 69 experimental disruptive children aged 6-12 on placement in the resource-room programme compared to 34 and then 48 'control' children who remained in ordinary classes. The resource room itself operated a systematised work assignment procedure and a token economy. The pupils spent one or two periods per day in the resource room on a fairly inflexible basis, and the resource-room teachers had very little time for liaison with or support of ordinary classteachers. Furthermore, by no means all the children were really disruptive, and the reliability of the follow-up results is rendered somewhat doubtful by high sample attrition.

In the first year, the resource-programme group scored significantly higher than ordinary class controls on reading comprehension and arithmetic fundamentals. In the second year, this group scored higher than controls on reading vocabulary, total reading, arithmetic fundamentals and total arithmetic; there were substantial academic gains. At first-year follow-up, only the arithmetic fundamentals gain remained on comparison with controls, and at second-year follow-up, all academic gains had disappeared. On the behavioural side, in the first year the resource-room group behaved better than controls when in the resource room, but when in regular classes their behaviour was the same as the controls, although both groups showed some improvement. A similar finding for the second year reported no improvement in both groups, however. No behavioural gains were evident at either first or second follow-up.

Glavin (1973) comments: 'Since generalisation of [improved] behaviour was not achieved initially, the lack of significant findings on follow-up after full-time placement in regular classrooms comes with little surprise. The data provide another demonstration that conditions in the regular classroom must be changed to support behaviour learned in the resource room.' Unfortunately this study did not use generalisation strategies.

Summary

Part-time resource-room placement can produce substantial academic gains and improved behaviour in the resource room. However, the improved behaviour does not automatically generalise to the ordinary classes, and both academic and behavioural gains tend to disappear after two years. This emphasises the need for conditions in the ordinary classroom to be changed, and the concept of the resource room as a resource for teacher support and training is discussed.

9 TIME-OUT ROOMS

These are rooms or some small facility in the school where a pupil is assigned to 'cool off'. This may be for a pre-specified period or until acceptable behaviour is demonstrated by the pupil. Some systems expect the child to continue with classwork, supplied by the ordinary class-teacher, while others require that the child sit in silence and ponder. Garibaldi (1979) notes from his survey that reassignment to ordinary classes is not always based on established policies and criteria. In some cases the pupil returns to ordinary classes after a behavioural contract has been established.

Garibaldi notes that the location and physical space of the facility varies widely. Some are in central classroom areas, others next to the headteacher's office, and many in inconspicuous places such as on remote corridors, in a basement or in a portable classroom. In many cases this removal of a pupil from the normal flow of activities and peers is a deliberate part of the strategy. All time-out facilities are for very short-term use.

There are descriptions of such facilities in UK schools. Westmacott (1980) refers to a 'remove room' manned by senior staff. Rabinowitz (1975) notes that in some schools an ordinary classroom may be set aside as an 'individual work centre' supervised by senior and/or experienced members of staff, where disruptive pupils may be sent to work quietly on tasks set by their normal teachers. Baxter (1976) described the operation of such a scheme in a school in North-east England, where it was termed the 'rehabilitation system'. In this case, however, children were sometimes withdrawn for as long as a week. The system was flexible, was not a way for pupils to avoid work, and did not occur in an identifiable single place, as the pupils on 'rehab' reported to the senior staff member covering the system for any one period at that teacher's usual base. There were difficulties in ensuring an adequate flow of work from subject teachers. The DES (1978a) describe a school which set up a time-out room, manned all day, to which any disruptive child could be sent *with* school work by a head of department. After three weeks so few pupils had been sent that the scheme was disbanded.

The essential concept of time-out, from whence it draws its name, derives from learning theory. The assumption is that the disruptive student must be getting something out of being disruptive (e.g. attention, peer group status, avoidance of work, etc.). Therefore the best way to reduce the disruptive behaviour should be by removing the student to 'time-out from reinforcement' — away from those things which are re-inforcing the disruptive behaviour.

Of course it can be argued that on the pupil's return to the original situation, the same 'reinforcers' will again operate, and disruptive be-haviour will recur. However, this may not happen if the pupil is aware that any recurrence will again automatically result in 'time-out'. It is obviously essential that 'time-out from reinforcement' is just that — it is no use whatsoever removing the pupil to a situation where alternative 'reinforcers' are available. Having a pupil sit outside the headteacher's office where he/she can act the fool and chat to passers-by is not going to help the situation. Also, Plummer (1977) shows that for some children time-out can actually be rewarding, if they have a great need to escape from the stressful situation resulting from their disruptive behaviour. Time-out is not intended to be punishing, to be experienced as highly unpleasant and aversive by the pupil. However, it does involve removal from all the factors tending to reinforce disruptive behaviour. These latter may well be different for different pupils. A further implication of this kind of analysis is that for such pupils, the rewards for conform-ing behaviour in the classroom must by definition be less than the rein-forcement for disruptive behaviour. As well as removal from the latter, the problem can obviously also be tackled by increasing the supply of the former.

There is very substantial evidence on the effectiveness of 'time-out' with disruptive and aggressive behaviour, but relatively little of this concerns adolescents in ordinary secondary schools. Sachs (1973), Bostow and Bailey (1969), Walker *et al.* (1968), Hawkins *et al.* (1967), Forehand and MacDonough (1975), Lovitt and Curtiss (1969), Tyler and Brown (1967), White *et al.* (1972), Burchard and Barrera (1972), etc., all found time-out to be effective. Drabman and Spitalnik (1973) found time-out effective and specific in action with children aged 9-11 years in classes in psychiatric institutions.

Various studies have investigated the effects of different durations of time-out. Burchard and Barrera (1972) found 30 minutes duration to be more effective than five minutes duration. However, illustrating the need for consistency, Kendall *et al.* (1975) found that five minutes time-out suppressed verbal aggression and out-of-area behaviour and moderately reduced physical aggression when presented prior to 30 minute time-out duration, but the five minutes time-out actually in-creased disruptive behaviour after the children had been exposed to the

30 minute duration. (This was in a residential recreation situation with 30 boys aged 9-14.) White *et al.* (1972) found similar results, while demonstrating that even one minute time-out could be fairly effective, provided it was used before exposure to longer durations of time-out. Kendall *et al.* (1975) found a similar 'sequence effect' with 30 adolescent delinquents. It seems clear that the effectiveness of short time-outs will be diminished if a longer duration has previously been employed.

Other parameters of time-out and their relationship to effectiveness have been studied (Hobbs and Forehand, 1977), but unfortunately very few of these studies have focused upon disruptive adolescents. However, there is evidence with other populations that: (1) the use of time-out as an intermittent or random intervention can be as effective as using it for every occurrence of the problem behaviour (this is not the same as using it in some lessons but not others!), especially for low-rate behaviours; (2) fixed-duration time-out may be less effective in some circumstances than contingent-release time-out (i.e. release from time-out achieved by the students showing acceptable behaviour). The latter condition also tended to produce better behaviour during time-out; (3) for time-out to be effective, the natural environment (i.e. classroom) must be reinforcing. Time-out imposed in an impoverished natural environment is of very doubtful effectiveness; (4) time-out involving complete removal of the offender from the situation is more effective than isolating or ignoring the child within the situation.

Pease and Tyler (1979) describe the use of time-out with 15 primary-aged pupils in a special class, where the problem pupil could determine the duration of the time-out. Self-regulation proved just as effective as teacher-stipulation of time-out duration. (Lovitt and Curtiss (1969) had previously found self-determination of reinforcement *more* effective than teacher-specification in improving academic work-rates, while Glynn (1970) and Felixbrod and O'Leary (1973) later found no difference in effectiveness between the two for this application.)

Webster (1976) offers an interesting case study of a 13-year-old boy in an ordinary school whose 'extremely wild and uncontrollable episodes of acting-out behaviour' had resulted in, among other things, the hospitalisation of two peer victims with head injuries. Utilising time-out, over a period of seven weeks, the child's average daily number of aggressive assaults fell from five to zero. In addition, attention, participation and work-rate in class increased, although this had not been targeted. Webster concludes that time-out can be a sufficiently intensive aversive event of itself to alter some types of deviant behaviour even without the additional direct application of positive reinforcers to give the child an incentive to increase acceptable behaviours incompatible with the problem behaviour.

Summary

There is substantial evidence that time-out rooms can be an effective means of curtailing disruptive behaviour. Various considerations in maximising the effectiveness of time-out are discussed. Methodical and consistent usage is likely to be necessary to ensure effectiveness, and lack of this may actually worsen the problem behaviour. Intermittent and self-regulated time-out have also been found to be effective.

10 CRISIS ROOMS/TEACHERS

The concept of the 'crisis teacher' who operates in, from or around a 'crisis room' is largely owed to Morse (1965, 1966). Morse sees the crisis teacher as able to mount 'immediate school rescue operations'. 'This teacher must really know curriculum, be steeped in remedial teaching techniques, and be skilled in life-space interviewing. The space provided may include a small classroom with a pleasant anteroom; books and materials of all sorts are at hand.' 'The crisis teacher does not have a regular group. Pupils may come and go, sometimes on a more or less regular basis as seems advisable, but often on an episodic basis when specific pressure accumulates.' Unfortunately Morse never clarifies what constitutes a 'crisis' and quite how the 'crisis teacher' would deal with it — he states 'the work which goes on is determined by the pupil's problem' and 'in crisis teaching, the teacher has to take a broad humanistic approach'; 'the crisis teacher is trained to take the child wherever he is and however he is and work with him in whatever way one can'.

Alachua County Schools (1975) tried out this model. Their 'crisis teachers' also acted as consultants to ordinary classteachers. It was found that there were considerable problems of role unclarity and feeling within schools that duplication of services was occurring. The crisis teacher needed to be exceptionally competent for the system to work, and there was the constant danger of the crisis teacher unwittingly positively reinforcing disruptive behaviour. Very close relationships between the crisis teacher and ordinary classteachers were found to be a prerequisite.

It would appear that 'crisis teachers' would largely depend on counselling to effect behaviour change in the pupil. Unfortunately, the evidence on the effectiveness of this approach, especially with disruptive/acting-out pupils, suggests the results are very rarely better than spontaneous remission (Levitt, 1957, 1963; Levitt *et al.*, 1959; Eysenck, 1960; Truax and Carkhuff, 1967; Eisenberg, 1969; Rachman, 1971; Robins, 1973; Hewett and Blake, 1973, etc.). *Group* counselling has been claimed to improve academic performance but not social behaviour in secondary school pupils (Mezzano, 1968; Baymur and Patterson, 1960), but the generalisability of these results seems doubtful. Mezzano, for instance, based his study on *volunteers* for counselling, and found that children who had individual as well as group counselling did worse than those solely exposed to group counselling, and that the difference in academic gains was not present at the end of the counselling programme, but only appeared ten weeks later. Baymur and Patterson found that both group and individual counselling improved subjects' grade-points, but that group counselling was more effective in this respect. Neither of these studies had subjects who were disruptive, however.

More encouragingly, positive evaluation results from group therapy along Rogerian lines with difficult pupils are reported by Kolvin *et al.* (1981) in the UK. However, the organisation of group counselling as a response to a 'crisis' is clearly likely to leave something to be desired in terms of immediacy, and the data from the Kolvin *et al.* (1981) study are reported in more detail in Chapter 17: 'Pupil Training'.

Garibaldi (1979) notes that in Louisiana counselling takes place *after* school. He also mentions a concept perhaps related to the 'crisis teacher' — that of a school Ombudsperson, who would mediate in conflicts between students and teachers or disputes between teachers, parents and administrators. He notes from his survey that this kind of resource person has been 'tried in many areas, but very few currently remain'.

Summary

It is unclear what 'crisis teachers' might do. Various disadvantages of this model have been found, but there is no adequate evaluation. Without a clearer conceptual structure and job description, evaluation is unlikely to be even possible. In so far as 'crisis teachers' depend on 'client-centred' individual counselling, they are likely to be ineffective, since there is very little evidence that such counselling is any more effective than spontaneous remission with disruptive pupils. However, one UK study has shown Rogerian *group* counselling to have a positive long-term effect on the behaviour of disruptive pupils, albeit with little immediate effect.

Part Four

IN-SCHOOL PERSONNEL RESOURCES

11 SUPPORT TEACHERS

A support teacher based within one secondary school would not offer regular part-time long-term tuition (resource-room concept), would not offer the constant availability of removal of disruptive pupils from the ordinary class (time-out concept), or rush about responding in some way to 'crises' ('crisis teacher' concept). This is not to say that a support teacher would not partially operate in direct contact with disruptive pupils, whether for short-term part-time tuition in or out of the regular class, for intensive individual counselling, or for contracting or contingency dispensation. However, 'support' could also take the form of pupil observation, problem clarification, behaviour modification programme design, monitoring and evaluation, more general consultation with, and reinforcement and encouragement of, ordinary teachers, and so on. Clearly, any teacher taking on these latter modes of operation would need high status, credibility and authority with respect to their colleagues.

Few UK schools can afford the 'luxury' of this kind of in-school resource person, and much of the literature in the area refers to an itinerant or peripatetic support teacher service, which is considered in Chapter 14. However, there is evidence (Coates, 1977) that many teachers feel a need for support, although to whom they are prepared to admit this may vary. Some 70 per cent of teachers felt a need for a form of counselling service for *staff*, and this was even more so with probationary teachers. Coates describes the staff support and in-service training role of a 'staff tutor'.

Lane (1978) describes a self-structuring and self-evaluation procedure for an itinerant support teacher which would also be valuable here. Upon deciding to involve themselves in a particular case, the support teachers: (1) make an initial definition of the problem in behavioural terms; (2) make baseline observations of frequency of occurrence of problem behaviour; (3) make an analysis of precipitating factors; (4) formulate initial intervention hypotheses; (5) negotiate to what behavioural changes the participants in the problem situation are prepared to contract; (6) monitor operation of agreed programme; (7) evaluate outcomes of intervention; (8) stipulate further objectives designed to ensure maintenance of gains; (9) negotiate agreement on these; (10) continue monitoring. Thus each 'support intervention' is evaluated within itself, in terms of its own objectives.

This 'problem-solving' model is very similar to that used effectively by Stratford and Cameron (1979) in secondary schools. In the USA, Cantrell and Cantrell (1977) describe 10 support teachers working in a similar way with 183 cases in one year, using a 'heuristic problem-solving' approach involving the detailed delineation of steps in the intervention and the setting of behavioural objectives. Unfortunately, they do not offer any concrete evaluative data, but it seems clear that if this system is carefully followed, positive outcomes are arrived at quicker than would otherwise be the case.

Gloss (1968) refers to an 'Experimental School Adjustment Programme' in Ohio which was based on support teachers involving themselves in intensive one-to-one counselling with pupils, in-service training for classteachers, and closer liaison with pupils' homes. Volunteer teacher aides were also utilised. Unfortunately no detailed evaluative data are cited. Gloss commented as long ago as 1968 that 'supportive' programmes were increasing faster than 'unit'-based programmes.

Jenkins and Mayhall (1976) noted that with primary-age learning disabled children, both direct teaching of the child by the resource teacher and indirect service by consultation with the ordinary classteacher resulted in increased word recognition skills, compared to unserved controls, but the former resulted in greater increases. The optimum time input for the two modes of operation is obviously likely to differ however, and this result may not reflect on cost-effectiveness. Nor is it clear whether this result has any relevance to secondary-age disruptive children.

Tennessee State DOMH (1975) provide a substantial evaluation of the fourth year's activities of their support teacher programme, which largely trained ordinary teachers to deal with the behavioural difficulties of elementary and junior high school children in the normal school environment, using the Cantrells' 'heuristic' model of operation. Evaluation results are noted to show that behavioural objectives set by support teachers were met, and that parents were supportive of the programme. It was noted that *intensive* consultative input and evaluative feedback was needed for the support teacher teams to become optimally effective. Summarisation of evaluation data in situations where each involvement has its own idiosyncratic objectives is, of course, very difficult. However, this report does suggest that support teaching, if done well, works.

Kolvin *et al.* (1981) report encouraging evaluation results from a programme of Rogerian-style 'group therapy' operated with problem pupils in secondary schools in the North-east of England. The initiation and maintenance of such groups could be one of the functions of a relevantly trained and experienced support teacher. The evaluation data are reported in detail in Chapter 17.

The only other remotely relevant UK work is evaluative studies of the West Sussex scheme of part-time therapy groups in primary schools (Labon, 1974; Cook *et al.*, 1979; Cook, 1980). This kind of direct service role could be undertaken by an in-school support teacher for one or more groups. The concept is not dissimilar from ILEA's 'nurture groups' (Chapter 7), except the Sussex groups operate for only two quarter-day sessions weekly for the average child, over a period ranging from a few weeks to a year or more. The groups are activity-orientated. Labon (1974) reports that after three years' operation of the programme, headteachers reported seeing improvement in the children, but Bristol Social Adjustment Guide scores showed no significant differences. Cook *et al.* (1979) unfortunately utilised 'controls' whose comparability is in some doubt. Some improvement in being 'on task' is reported, but academic or attainment gains are not reported. Some lowering in the frequency of aggressive acts is noted, but it is not stated whether this was significant. Cook (1980) is equally vague, referring to 'encouraging trends' — after nine years of operation of the programme.

Finally, McDonald *et al.* (1970) report on the significant improvement of school attendance in 15- and 16-year-old chronic non-attenders by 'contingency counselling' by paraprofessional aides. This is basically the operation of a behaviour modification system, with additional non-routine rewards and punishments being made contingent upon attendance or non-attendance. The identification, securing and manipulation of such contingencies requires time and planning, and could well constitute part of the function of a support teacher.

Summary

There is very little directly relevant evaluative evidence on in-school support teachers. However, there is some evidence that, provided such teachers operate within a very clearly structured, behaviourally oriented problem-solving model, a high proportion of casework objectives can be met. Alternatively, one UK study has demonstrated positive long-term (but not short-term) effects from group counselling.

12 PARAPROFESSIONALS

The use of paraprofessionals as 'teacher aides' or in direct service to disruptive children has quite a long (documented) history in both the USA and the UK.

In the US, Ward and Tikunoff (1979) provide a substantial analysis of how the introduction of paraprofessionals into the classroom might affect the social dynamic, but offer no evaluative data. Cowen *et al.* (1968) describe how six retired persons were recruited, trained and paid a nominal fee to work with disruptive children in primary schools during twice-weekly activity periods of 35-40 minutes. The pensioners attended 100 per cent and enjoyed their work, and the children's class-teachers felt the children had improved. Little hard data is provided, however. Cowen (1968) reports on a more detailed study, where three groups were compared during a five-month programme: (1) four house-wives working with 17 disruptive children for several 30-minute activity periods per week; (2) college students doing likewise, but mostly after school; (3) control group. The housewives produced significant improvement in class according to teacher rating scales, while the college students' group was little different from the controls. This study was also with elementary pupils. Cowen *et al.* (1972) sought to determine whether 36 children seen 2 to 5 years earlier (in elementary school) by non-professional aides for school maladaptation problems, maintained the short-term programme gains over time. Rather curiously, this was attempted by interviewing the children's parents. In retrospect, the majority of the parents felt their children had improved on seven out of eight rating factors. However, no control group was available, and the results were analysed in a way which makes it difficult to determine whether they were significantly different from spontaneous remission rates.

On a completely different basis, McDonald *et al.* (1970) selected 'community people' for each of six 15-year-old chronic non-attenders, who had already developed a relationship with the student outside of school. The paraprofessionals set up contingency contracts with their students, stipulating certain rewards which could be gained by attending school (e.g. access to pool hall, weekend privileges, etc.). Using a reversal experimental design, the effectiveness of the approach is clearly demonstrated, and two replications of the study yielded similar results.

This programme bears great similarity to the work of Tharp and Wetzel (1969), discussed elsewhere.

In the UK, Lansdown reported in 1971 on the use of 'welfare assistants' as one-to-one activity-based part-time workers with disruptive primary children in ordinary schools. Five such assistants, supervised by a psychologist, operated in this way. Although some encouraging results are cited, no hard evaluative data is presented.

Presland (1973) notes that Wahler and Erickson (1969) and Breyer *et al.* (1971) found encouraging results from non-professional personnel trained to operate behaviour modification programmes in classrooms. He describes the use in infant and junior schools of a paraprofessional trained in behaviour modification techniques, whose substantial success with two particular cases is described.

Hulbert *et al.* (1977) describe the teacher-aide programme piloted in six junior schools in Newcastle-on-Tyne. These teacher-aides implemented behaviour 'shaping' (modification) programmes as well as offering 'nurturance' (see Boxall, 1973). Hulbert *et al.* mention some of the practical problems and how these were resolved. Initial subjective impressions from both teachers and aides were of improvement in the 'target' disruptive children. More detailed evaluative data showed this trend only reached statistical significance at overall long-term follow-up (Kolvin *et al.*, 1981). Some improvement was evident at home as well as at school.

Summary

The use of housewives, pensioners, neighbours, welfare assistants, etc. as activity leaders, nurturers and behaviour modifiers with disruptive children in primary schools is a well-established practice in both the UK and the USA. Several favourable short-term evaluations are reported, although the data are often neither detailed nor concrete.

Paraprofessionals in the community have been effective in increasing school attendance in 15-year-old chronic truants, by the use of behaviour modification techniques (contingency contracting). However, paraprofessional programmes for disruptive children in secondary school are uncommon in the literature, although why this is so, especially in the case of comprehensive community schools, is not clear.

13 VOLUNTEERS

Adult Volunteers

Programmes utilising adult volunteers and those using paraprofessionals are often distinguishable only by the latter's involving payment. In some cases, it is unclear whether the adults were paid or not, and the division between Chapter 12 and this first half of Chapter 13 may be somewhat arbitrary.

Allen *et al.* (1976) review the literature on various adult 'companion' programmes. One of the first of these was that of Zax *et al.* (1966), which utilised housewives. Cowen *et al.* (1966) used volunteer college students as companions for disturbed children in elementary schools. Seventeen 'enthusiastic' undergraduates, given no special training, failed to produce significant changes in teacher ratings of child behaviour in class (as compared to a control group) in the course of a two-month programme. A study of a similar operation over a five-month period (Cowen *et al.*, 1969) did show improved teacher and companion ratings.

On a less optimistic note, Stern *et al.* (1971) used three adult females as companions for five pre-school children, but their evaluation was aborted when the control group got out of hand. Smith (1969) also used housewives, who spent time with the children on 'talking and academic tasks'. No significant improvement in behaviour or performance as compared to a control group occurred. Goodman (1972) utilised male college students as companions to 88 11- and 12-year-old boys. The companions were carefully selected and underwent substantial training. A client-centred, unstructured, one-to-one approach was used, and unfortunately this was found to result in, if anything, a deterioration in the children's behaviour when compared to the control group.

More encouragingly, Allen *et al.* (1976) found that a 'companion' programme with 9- and 10-year-old children resulted in the improvement of 19 out of 20 'experimental' children in social interaction with peers, to the extent that they became virtually indistinguishable from 'normal'. Only 60 per cent of the controls improved and then not to the same extent. Teacher ratings of social behaviour and sociometric ratings by peers showed no change, although observation clearly indicated that the behaviour had changed.

Two further studies demonstrate, yet again, the utility and effectiveness of behavioural techniques. Fo and O'Donnell (1974) found that school attendance was increased when adult companions from the community were trained to use contingency management techniques. A control group also allocated 'companions', but not subject to contingency management, showed no improvement on this basis, but when contingency management was introduced to this group at a later date, improvements resulted here also. Fo and O'Donnell utilised similar techniques with a further six children who had other difficulties (of fighting, non-completion of homework and/or schoolwork, etc.), and demonstrated success here also. Patterson (1974), in work similar to that of Tharp and Wetzel (1969), reported a study with a 12-month follow-up showing improvement of boys with conduct problems in both home-based and classroom-centred programmes. Patterson was heavily involved in training non-professionals as behaviour-analytic change agents at the Oregon Research Institute.

The Ohio State Department of Education (1974) reports a substantial volunteer programme in nine school districts, where unpaid and untrained volunteers from the community worked with disturbed children in a one-to-one setting for two periods of 35-40 minutes weekly. There were simple volunteer selection criteria. The volunteers were asked to offer supportive relationships and success experiences, in the hope that this would improve the children's behaviour and academic attainment. Detailed evaluative data are not provided, but it is noted that the scheme was particularly helpful for immature/inadequate or shy/withdrawn children. Also, the more 'warm and understanding' the volunteer was, the better the children did. The service was considered a useful ancillary programme for children with 'mild disturbances'. A valuable list of management objectives for programme implementation is provided, as is a detailed list of practical problems encountered.

The Ohio comment that the system was 'cheap and flexible' is echoed by Cowen (1974), who in describing his three-year Primary Mental Health Project, which involved the use of non-professional aides to help maladapting primary-age pupils in 16 schools, noted that this programme was *10 times* cheaper than the traditional service delivery system.

Peer Volunteers

Anyone who is sceptical about expecting children to solve the problems of other children would do well to bear in mind the findings of Jenkins and Mayhall (1976), in whose study peer tuition of remedial reading to children with learning difficulties was found to be substantially superior to small group instruction by a teacher.

Comment was made in the introduction to this book that the 'within-child' model of disruptive behaviour is now widely acknowledged to be defunct, and manipulating peer influence on disruptive children within the situation where the disruption occurs would seem to be a promising avenue of enquiry. Graubard (1969a) refers to traditional 'clinical' methods of treating child disturbance as attempts to apply the 'artichoke technique' − i.e. 'peel off' the child from the natural situation. He discusses a range of research evidence emphasising the need to work with the existing group, and advocates an approach based on a combination of social psychology and learning theory.

Graubard (1969b) himself gives a good example of this approach, in a study of eight disruptive boys aged 10-12 in a special class. Points were made available to the disruptive children for rule-following and high work output, and these were exchanged for rewards for the whole group. The incidence of disruptive behaviour was reduced from 24 per cent to 10 per cent by these means. Other examples of the effectiveness of 'group reinforcement' are numerous. Walker and Hops (1973) demonstrated that social interaction with socially isolated children may be increased by structuring situations in which both withdrawn children and classroom peers are reinforced for increasing frequencies of reciprocal social behaviour. Nelson *et al.* (1973) successfully taught disruptive children in a residential camp programme to manage various aspects of assorted behaviour change programmes with their peers.

A variant of this technique is for the adult directly to reinforce the target child's peers for behaving in a certain way towards the disruptive pupil. For example, Kirby and Toler (1970) reinforced an isolated child's peers for verbally interacting with the withdrawn pupil.

Taking a rather different approach, Solomon and Wahler (1973) asked highly sociometrically ranked peers who had previously reinforced the disruptive behaviour of five 12-year-old boys to ignore certain specifically defined disruptions and respond positively only to study behaviour. They obliged, and disruptive behaviour reduced substantially. Lovitt *et al.* (1973) found similar results with the same procedure.

Csapo (1972) provided another example of direct reinforcement by peers. She asked selected peers either to record the target pupils' behaviour or to model the socially appropriate behaviour for six disruptive children of primary age. The peer 'behavioural engineers' also dispensed token reinforcement, and disruptive behaviour reduced in frequency, and continued to decline even after the intervention programme had ended. Long and Madsen (1975) used 5-year-olds as reinforcing agents to modify the inappropriate classroom behaviour of 3-year-olds!

Strain *et al.* (1976) review much of the work in this field, but unfortunately the bulk of the studies refer only to primary-aged children. Strain *et al.* point out that the utilisation of peer volunteers gets round the problems facing adult-directed behaviour modification programmes, namely: (1) inconsistency between different teachers; (2) much antisocial behaviour occurs when the pupil is out of the teacher's sight; (3) adults are in short supply in schools, whereas children are not; (4) behaviour changes engineered by teachers may not endure in the teacher's absence. In support of this contention, they cite work by Surratt *et al.* (1969), who found that children trained to attend to a task by a peer remained at task so long as the trainer peer was present, and that this continued even after the peer-reinforcement conditions were removed. Walker and Buckley (1972) have used peers to facilitate maintenance and generalisation of behavioural gains in disruptive primary-age pupils returning to ordinary schools.

Several investigators have demonstrated the value of involving peers as models to assist in behaviour modification efforts to change classmates' social behaviour. Much research has shown that children are likely to imitate a peer whom they observe to be the recipient of reinforcement (Bandura *et al.*, 1963; Broden *et al.*, 1970b; Carnine *et al.*, 1968; Christy, 1975; Clark, 1965; Geshuri, 1972; Kazdin, 1973, etc.) and teachers may here have a way of utilising the target child's peers in a programme of behavioural change without the peers ever actually 'volunteering'.

Strain *et al.* (1976) also point out that there is no evidence that the use of peers as behaviour modifiers results in any detriment to the peers. Indeed, there is some evidence (Siegel and Steinman, 1975) that such programmes can result in improvement in rates of desirable behaviour in the peer-reinforcing agents as well. Glavin and Quay (1969) report that using peer tutors aged 6-10 years resulted in very substantial gains in reading not only for the tutees but also for the peer tutors. Gains of up to 2.6 years of reading age in a five-month period were found.

Nor should the ability of children reliably to implement these strategies be underestimated, as the aforementioned study of Long and Madsen (1975) demonstrates. McLaughlin and Malaby (1975) describe the successful training of elementary school children in the designing, implementation and evaluation of behaviour change projects with their peers. Quay and Glavin (1970) report the use of an immature 7-year-old as a peer tutor using behavioural techniques.

However, relatively few of these impressive studies have actually focused on disruptive adolescents within the ordinary secondary school, and few have any evidence of long-term duration of behavioural gains. Nevertheless, strategies for maintenance and generalisation of gains are much more readily to hand from behavioural technology than is the case with interventions based on other bodies of knowledge.

The other major area in this field is that of Peer Counselling. Garibaldi (1979) notes the existence of various attempts to create a 'positive peer culture', whereby students are trained in fundamentals of guidance counselling and then counsel peers who display behavioural problems. Irving (1975) describes a project where adolescents were paid to counsel younger problem children from four elementary schools. Bower (1972) describes a peer-counselling programme in secondary schools, involving a substantial amount of training for the volunteer counsellors. Enthusiasm on the part of the participants and a large number of requests for service are reported, but no hard evaluative data are available. McWilliams and Finkel (1973) used under-achieving high school students to counsel shy, withdrawn children. Teacher ratings of the counselled children showed improvement in the counselled group as compared to a control group. Evaluative effort of even this degree of sophistication seems unusual in the area of peer counselling, however, and as was noted in earlier sections, counselling by professional adults is of doubtful effectiveness.

Summary

Studies of the effectiveness of adult volunteers show very mixed results, with as many failures as successes. Adult volunteers have been successful with disruptive primary-age children and with immature/inadequate children. Adult volunteers using behavioural techniques have been successful with a variety of problem behaviours.

Peer volunteer programmes using behavioural techniques show substantial evidence of effectiveness. Peer group contingencies have proved effective with disruptive children in primary-school and residential settings. Reinforcement by peers has demonstrated effectiveness with disruptive children in both primary and secondary age ranges. The utilisation of peer modelling has been found effective in a variety of situations. Only one or two studies give evidence of long-term duration of gains, but as behavioural techniques do not purport to be a one-off 'treatment', this is unsurprising. The main alternative model for utilising peers, peer counselling, has been considerably less well researched, and there is no evidence that it is effective with disruptive children.

Part Five

EXTERNAL PERSONNEL RESOURCES

14 ITINERANT SUPPORT TEACHERS

Itinerant support teachers are able to act in similar ways to in-school support teachers (see Chapter 11), but would obviously be thinner on the ground and have less time available per problem. They would have the disadvantage of not knowing schools so intimately, but the possible advantage of greater objectivity thereby. The problem-solving strategies of Lane (1978), Cantrell and Cantrell (1977) and Stratford and Cameron (1979) would be of even greater value within a situation of such limited resource availability.

Chazan (1973) describes the operation in Scandinavia of Special Education Centres, staffed by psychologists, social workers and specialist teachers of handicapped pupils, who offer advice and help to ordinary schools, back this with resources from their resource bank and offer a peripatetic teaching service where necessary.

In Britain, Griffiths (1980, 1981) and his colleagues have described the operation of their 'Special Education Team': six teachers working solely on an itinerant casework basis with disruptive secondary pupils in a northern authority's 23 comprehensive schools. The team do not withdraw any children from the ordinary school for teaching, although some disruptive children are taught on a one-to-one basis by a peripatetic teacher in the ordinary school for some lessons. The team works very closely with the psychologists and has strong administrative support from the authority.

Methods of working vary from case to case, and there is an emphasis on flexibility. There is an attempt to maximise objectivity and not side with any particular client in a situation. Initial data-collection may involve meeting with all the staff who teach a problematic pupil, using sociometric analyses, inventories or rating scales, and/or making observations in class. An attempt is made to negotiate an agreed problem definition with the referring agency. Action may involve support and advice to individual teachers, co-ordinating a support team of teachers, senior staff and possibly peers around the problem child in school, direct counselling and/or contingency contracting with the problem pupil by the specialist teacher, sometimes directly teaching the problem child or children in the ordinary school, either out of or within the ordinary classes. There is a great emphasis laid upon not allowing the problem child to become too dependent on the SET teacher. The periods over which direct teaching has occurred with children range from three days to one academic year. Some parent liaison is undertaken where relevant.

Unfortunately little hard evaluative evidence is available, although attempts are made to specify objectives for each case. However, it is clear that on the criterion which separate units for disruptive children most commonly claim to espouse, i.e. return to ordinary school, this system has a 100 per cent success rate, since the children are not withdrawn in the first place. Griffiths *et al.* (1981) also point out that pupils are often quickly reintegrated to a normal timetable, can follow the normal curriculum, are not 'labelled' and are not placed in mutually reinforcing association with other disruptive pupils. Further change within school systems is encouraged in addition to change within the disruptive pupils.

Harrison (1980) reports on a superficially similar team in another northern authority which has evolved rather differently. These 20 teachers were also nominally intended to be a support resource to ordinary schools, but the teachers were made responsible to the heads of special schools. These teachers actually appear to do very little support, advice or programming, and tend either to teach the children directly in the ordinary schools on a peripatetic basis, or to channel them in large numbers towards special schools, despite several secondary schools having their own in-school units. There appear to be difficulties of referral and casework control and a lack of clarity as to role and function.

Kolvin *et al.* (1976, 1981) describe a system of itinerant social work consultation and support for the parents and teachers of disruptive pupils in both junior and senior schools. The social workers advised the teachers about child management, optimum academic pressure and extra-curricular activities, as well as providing information about the home circumstances of problem pupils. The social workers tried to link school and home as well as working on problems in the home. Unfortunately the detailed evaluative evidence was not at all encouraging (Kolvin *et al.*, 1981).

Turning to US studies, Alachua County Schools noted that their itinerant support programme had been less effective than their special class (Chapter 7), and resource-room (Chapter 8) programmes, but of course it was substantially cheaper per pupil served. No detailed information on cost-effectiveness is given. The Alachua itinerant team 'supported classteachers, mobilised community resources, worked with parents and promoted academic skills'. The advantages were that the team formed an in-service training resource, helped ordinary classteachers to solve problems and served more students. The disadvantages were that the team was 'spread too thin', and did not manage to establish good relationships everywhere, remaining somewhat alienated from some ordinary schools.

In one of the best documented projects, Tharp and Wetzel (1969) described a large-scale consultation programme where behavioural technology experts advised 'mediators' (teachers and parents) about the management of difficult children. Significant improvements in both social and academic behaviours were reported in a large number of cases, coupled with improvement in behaviours other than target behaviours and long-term reductions in criminal offences.

On a different model, Bailey and Kackley (1976) described an attempt to reduce the number of suspensions in high and junior high schools, as compared to 'control' schools. There had been a 200 per cent increase in suspension over the preceding four years, and the evaluation criterion was simply a reduction in suspension rates. The PASS project operated by attempting to improve human communication and feelings of self-worth in the organisational context, and small group workshops, seminars, counselling and encounter-type groups for the *teachers* were mounted by psychologists and social workers. Time-out room workers were also employed. There is no way of determining the differential effectiveness of the various components of the programme. In the PASS high schools, suspensions did fall during the two years of programme operation, while control school suspension rates increased. In the PASS junior highs, suspensions did increase, but still significantly less so than was the case in the *control* schools. However, it is doubtful whether this result is generalisable to the British context, since the pre-PASS suspension rates were very high, at 1,766 suspensions for a student enrollment of 2,945 per year. It is pointed out that programme costs were very small per pupil.

Summary

Itinerant services which offer peripatetic teaching of disruptive children in the ordinary school can have a 100 per cent success rate on the evaluative criterion of 'return to ordinary school', given clear definition of role and function and appropriate channels of responsibility. While itinerant services may be less effective than special classes or resource rooms for the more severe cases, they are likely to be more cost-effective on the whole, and this would be particularly true in areas where there were few disruptive pupils. Again, systems using behavioural techniques provide the most detailed and most encouraging evaluative data. Alternatively, workshops aimed at improving intra-organisation communication have been found to reduce suspension rates in schools where these were previously very high.

15 CONSULTANTS

There is considerable overlap between the functions of an itinerant support teacher (Chapter 14) and a 'consultant'. However, a 'consultant' is likely to cover a much larger area or number of schools (i.e. be an even scarcer resource), and be restricted to problem clarification and advisory input about problem solution, having no direct teaching input to the child. This role has been alternatively labelled 'diagnostic-prescriptologist', the medical connotations of which are likely to be highly misleading and to create quite inappropriate expectations (Alachua County Schools, 1975).

Consultative services may be provided by advisory teachers, university departments, educational psychologists and a range of other professions. In the UK, the function is most commonly undertaken by educational psychologists, but in the USA a wide range of professionals and paraprofessionals may be involved in attempts to promote 'mental health' in a community by consultative endeavour.

Iscoe *et al.* (1967) and Pierce-Jones *et al.* (1968) studied consultation services to schools in the US. Using various questionnaire methods, they concluded that there was no evidence that the amount of consultation sought about a child related to the 'severity of his disorder', and that the main concern of teachers was seeking from the consultant confirmation of a decision already made. Although most teachers viewed the consultants favourably, supportive direct teaching services were favoured much more. (And, of course, cost much more.) During the consultation process, rapport and relationships between consultants and consultees improved, but few other positive results emerged.

Mannino and Shore (1972, 1975) reviewed the literature on the evaluation of consultation. Of a total of 35 studies, positive change of some kind was demonstrated in 24 (69 per cent) — the ubiquitous two-thirds again. Some 74 per cent of the studies showed change in the consultee, but only 58 per cent showed change in the eventual client. Many of the studies used paper and pencil measures of 'attitude' or other mentalistic artefacts rather than observations of behaviour, the consultation input varied enormously in type, intention, quality and intensity between the studies, and the more recent and better controlled studies have demonstrated change in the eventual client considerably more rarely. Nevertheless, of 12 studies focusing on client rather than

97

consultee outcome, 8 showed positive effects from consultation in excess of improvements in control groups.

Hunter and Ratcliffe (1968) compared the relative effectiveness of direct (therapeutically oriented) service and consultation to the primary caretakers from a mental health centre base. They found the majority of all clients showed improvement irrespective of type of service offered. Lewis (1970a, 1970b) reports a similar study, of counselling guidance workers operating in the two modes, but in this case neither approach made any difference to the sociometric status of the children or teachers' ratings of their level of adjustment.

Tobiessen and Shai (1971) found no difference in child improvement on teacher rating scales in a comparison of the effectiveness of individual and group consultation with teachers — even though the teachers markedly preferred the latter and it cost much less.

The studies of Cutler and McNeil (1966) and Friedlander (1968) suggest that consultation needs to be intensive if it is to have any effects, although again the use of paper and pencil 'measures' may be thought to leave some doubt as to the actual meaning of the results. However, intensiveness of consultation does not guarantee the required results. Tyler (1971), in a comparative study of the effectiveness of more intense with less intense consultation, found that while the teachers receiving intensive consultation were happier with it and felt they understood more, there was no evidence of their putting any more of the advice into practice than was the case with the less intensive consultation group. These results echo the Iscoe *et al.* (1967) and Pierce-Jones *et al.* (1968) findings. Schowengerdt *et al.* (1976) also found some evidence that the largest factor in teacher satisfaction with consultative services from psychologists was the quality of relationship the teachers enjoyed with the consultants.

Alachua County Schools (1975) report on their 'diagnostic-prescriptologists', purely advisory personnel who make recommendations, map out programmes, provide materials, devise record systems and suggest testing procedures, as well as liaising with parents. This system was found to be effective only with mildly disruptive children, and there were problems with some teachers feeling threatened by it.

Wright and Payne (1979) report on an evaluation of Psychological Service consultative casework in the UK. Questionnaires indicated that 62 per cent of 676 referrals over a five-year period had improved, but no control groups were used. Topping (1978) reports a similar casework follow-up. After less than a year, all but 11 per cent of the children had improved, but the teachers considered that in only 24 per cent of cases was this even partially due to the consultation received. Half of the teachers felt less worried and more confident as a result of the consultation, but only 35 per cent claimed to have carried out any of the recommended action.

By contrast, Patterson (1974) could afford the luxury of excluding non-cooperative clients from his research design, and offered extremely intensive consultation. His five-man team dealt with just 27 'conduct problem' boys in the home setting, and in 14 cases consultation was also offered to the school. Structured behavioural training with close individual follow-up was evaluated by direct observation, and significant decreases in disruptive behaviour were noted, which persisted at follow-up in both settings. Average time cost for family consultative interventions was 33½ hours, and for school interventions 30½ hours. Not all cases improved, but improvement rates were better than spontaneous remission. Patterson reports replications of these findings.

Topping (1977b) lists many other papers pertaining to the evaluation of the consultative activities of psychological services, but unfortunately hard evaluative data on the effectiveness of consultation in the area of disruptive adolescents are rare indeed.

An example of consultation from a different professional base is provided by Kolvin *et al.* (1981), who deployed six specially trained social workers in six secondary schools, to work during one academic year with both teachers and parents, with the aim of helping 147 identified children with adjustment problems. The social workers were to consult with teachers about the management of identified pupils and establish short-term casework programmes with the parents of these children. There was an emphasis on improving links between parents and teachers. The social workers had no direct contact with the children.

The teachers and parents reported some increase in understanding of the children's problems, but on more objective assessments there was little evidence of significant change in the children's adjustment. In retrospect, it might appear excessively optimistic to have expected changed behaviour in school to result from consultative input to teachers from a professional group outside the education service.

Summary

There is considerable evidence that teachers often enjoy the consultative relationship, but it seems that resulting behaviour change on their part is considerably less frequent, and consequent improvement in the children is even less frequently demonstrated, with some programmes failing even to reach spontaneous remission rate.

A few studies have demonstrated effectiveness relative to controls in terms of child improvements, but it seems clear that to be effective, consultation needs to be intensive and carefully structured and is most cost-effectively carried out in groups. It cannot be expected to be effective with the most severely disruptive children. The behavioural analysis framework again appears as a most promising approach. Consultation may often be little less effective than direct 'therapy' by outside agencies, but teachers naturally prefer the provision of supplementary direct teaching services, which of course is considerably more costly.

16 TEACHER TRAINING

In previous chapters reference has been made to the training of teachers in the management of disruptive behaviour, carried out individually and in groups by support teachers and consultants, as part of a wider programme of action. In this chapter, programmes which are totally directed towards the in-service training of teachers will be considered.

Minde and Werry (1968) invested 300 hours of psychiatric consultation, 1,500 hours of tutorial time and 200 hours of social worker time with teachers, but no subsequent changes in observed classroom behaviour were evident in the children in the experimental teachers' classes, as compared to a control group.

An interesting model for in-service training is described by Berger and Wigley (1980). This is termed the Teacher-Child Interaction Project and is operated by the Psychology Department at the Institute of Psychiatry, University of London, in conjunction with the Inner London Education Authority. Recording of teacher-child behaviour in the classroom is carried out by the teacher and/or an outside observer. The teacher then makes some change in teaching style or management method with the problem pupil, and further observations are made to evaluate the effectiveness of the experiment. The process continues until success is achieved. This procedure is, of course, very similar to the Lane (1978), Stratford and Cameron (1979), and Cantrell and Cantrell (1977) 'problem-solving' models, but in this case is taught to teachers on a course to which they are seconded. During the secondment, they are also taught how to teach the course, so that they can teach other teachers, and so on. However, no evaluation results have come to light.

Dering (1980) describes a preventative programme of Active Tutorial Work, designed to improve relationships, communications and modes of organisation within secondary schools. Schools contract in to a programme of in-school in-service training for teachers, wherein the teachers are allocated to small groups and undertake various developmental group work exercises. Individuals are encouraged to examine their own behaviour in groups and become more aware of group processes, and as their awareness increases, apply their new insights to the classroom teaching situation. It is hoped that teachers become able to sense and avert crises before they occur. Teaching is conceptualised as effective group leadership. To facilitate this, the teachers then hold hour-long tutorial sessions with their classes on a weekly basis. A second level of training for the teachers, focusing on transactional analysis, is proposed. Unfortunately no evaluation data are yet available.

This programme bears some resemblance to the aforementioned PASS programme reported by Bailey and Kackley (1976), which was found to be effective in reducing the number of school suspensions, albeit from a previously astronomical level.

HUMRRO (1974) describe a more varied INSET programme (to 183 primary school teachers) which covered contingency management, parent counselling and communication skills. Evaluation was carried out by specially trained classroom observers and the use of standardised tests of attainment. Teachers who had received contingency management training produced more desired changes in student behaviour than teachers who had not received such training, but no significant differences in academic attainment were found.

Also with a behavioural flavour, Brownsmith *et al.* (1976) describe a Behaviour Management Training Programme for 86 regular and special teachers. By verbal input and role-play, teachers were trained in the use of various management strategies, e.g. redirection, interpretation, consequences, incentive manipulation, etc., which seemed to owe as much to the theories of Fritz Redl as to behavioural technology. Evaluation was by 'attitude' analysis, tests of knowledge and the teachers' self-report of their subsequent frequency of use of the techniques. There is no information concerning the impact of any teacher usage of these strategies on the children.

There are a number of well-known writers who manage to blend intimate awareness of the reality of classroom practice with a sound theoretical model and a basis of empirical research, most notably Gnagey (1975), Kounin (1970) and Robertson (1981). Their work would seem ideal as a framework for the in-service training of teachers, but no reports of evaluations of such endeavours emerged from the literature search.

The vast majority of reports in this area refer to the training of teachers in strictly behavioural techniques. Many review articles summarise the innumerable studies which have chronicled the success of behavioural techniques in reducing disruptive behaviour, increasing academic behaviour and increasing academic attainment (e.g. Clarizio and Yelon, 1967; O'Leary and Drabman, 1971; Altman and Linton, 1971; Sherman and Bushell, 1974; O'Leary and O'Leary, 1976; Nietzel *et al.*, 1977; Macmillan and Kolvin, 1977; Harrop, 1978; O'Leary, 1978; Presland, 1980). While the majority of studies refer to primary-school settings, a substantial number have demonstrated success with adolescent disruptives.

Presland (1980) cites eight behavioural studies which have demonstrated reduced disruption and increased work rate with children aged 12-14, and seven demonstrating this with the 15-19 age range. Studies have also demonstrated the effectiveness of behaviour modification in reducing physical assaults by a 13-year-old and increasing school attendance in 15/16-year-old chronic truants (Webster, 1976, and McDonald *et al.*, 1970, respectively).

Rosenfeld (1972) and Page and Edwards (1978) found behavioural strategies effective in secondary school classrooms. McAllister *et al.* (1969) and Warner *et al.* (1979) describe the effective use of social reinforcers by teachers with secondary-age pupils. Schmidt and Ulrich (1969) demonstrated successful use of group contingencies for a whole class, and this approach was taken further by Medland and Stachnik (1972), Harris and Sherman (1973) and Warner *et al.* (1979) who effectively used variants of the 'good behaviour game' with whole classes. White-Blackburn *et al.* (1977) describe the successful use of behavioural contracting with secondary-age pupils, while Main and Munro (1977) report the effective use of a fully-fledged token economy in a junior high school. Mention should also be made of the studies of Broden *et al.* (1971); Solomon and Wahler (1973); Hall *et al.* (1968a, 1970); Schumaker *et al.* (1977); Marlowe *et al.* (1978); and Glynn (1970).

Some criticism has been levelled at behaviour modification techniques on the grounds that their effects are specific and temporary. Still, at least they have effects. It is certainly true that a relatively small proportion of the very large number of studies of the effectiveness of behaviour modification have included data on generalisation of 'intervention' effects to other situations, or long-term follow-up data on duration of gains after termination of the intervention. To a large extent this is, of course, because behavioural psychology carries no implication that gains from contingency management *will* generalise to situations or times where contingencies are not managed. If behaviour is a function of its consequences, of course it will tend to reflect the contingencies which prevail in the situation in which the child in question currently finds himself, rather than those of a situation the child left some time ago.

While, contrary to this theory, behavioural gains do sometimes inexplicably and spontaneously generalise and transfer across situations, this certainly cannot be relied upon. If transfer and generalisation are required, then programming must be developed to ensure that this occurs.

There are several studies which have demonstrated generalisation, and Wildman and Wildman (1975), Presland (1981) and Kolvin *et al.* (1981) cite some of these and give useful guidelines for ensuring that generalisation does occur. Kauffmann *et al.* (1977) reported that 36 out of 42 studies in which follow-up data were reported showed effective maintenance.

It is concluded in many reviews (e.g. in Duke, 1979) that behavioural techniques have much promise in the classroom, although rather more thought and effort are required for their successful use in secondary schools than in primary schools. However, this latter disadvantage can be ameliorated by using the peer group, parents or the problem child himself as monitors of the programme (see Chapters 13, 17 and 18 for fuller details). Macmillan and Kolvin (1977) conclude 'behaviour modification is an important tool in the teacher's range of management and teaching strategies'.

While this may no longer be in dispute among many sections of the educational community, the question of how effective in-service training is as a vehicle for changing teacher strategies and thereby changing child behaviour is a slightly different question. That success is not guaranteed is noted by McNamara and Harrop (1979), who reported on workshops involving 100 secondary school teachers, of whom only 6 subsequently carried out a behaviour modification programme in which success was both claimed by the teacher and supported by numerical data collected by the teacher. Wheldall and Austin (1980) counter this with an example of successful training, and provide a useful discussion of the practical difficulties involved.

McKeown (1975) reports on a 6 x ½-hour training course for four groups of five elementary teachers. Even with such a brief training period, post-course tests showed knowledge increments and before and after classroom observations showed reductions in disruptiveness. By contrast, Goodwin (1966) investigated the effectiveness of training teachers in reinforcement techniques by individual consultation and group meetings, without finding any significant success.

Various different training formats have been used. Krumboltz and Goodwin (1966) devised a training film. Other investigators have gone into the classroom and provided signals to the teacher for various contingencies (Hall *et al.*, 1968b; Becker *et al.*, 1967). Many programmes make some provision for didactic training, often via a seminar format (Barclay, 1967; Becker *et al.*, 1967; Haughton, 1968; Thomas *et al.*, 1968). Madsen and Madsen (1973) and Barclay (1970) found supplementing verbal means with role-play and modelling effective, while

Barclay also used techniques of micro-teaching, discrimination learning and behaviour shaping. Videotape feedback has been utilised by Hawkins (1974) and by Whitley (1971), who found it effective in eliciting increased teacher reinforcement of desired student behaviour, which resulted in improved student behaviour. However, Whitley's comparison group of teachers who had received video feedback but no explanatory input also increased their reinforcement of desirable student behaviour, although the behaviour of their students showed no change.

As Kolvin *et al.* (1981) point out, traditional instructional methods (lectures, discussions and other didactic exercises) are the most widely employed approach, although there is little reliable evidence that this component of training leads to actual application of behaviour techniques, as distinct from facilitating the acquisition of knowledge about such techniques. Opportunities for supervision of, feedback about and reinforcement concerning attempted *application* of the techniques, to supplement didactic procedures, have been shown to increase training effectiveness. There is evidence that the effectiveness of feedback from trainer to trainee is heightened by its immediacy. Praising teachers for praising their pupils has been shown to be more effective than merely telling teachers to do so. This explicit use of social reinforcement is as effective with teachers as it is with children. That frequent praise and feedback for the teacher are necessary to effect changed teacher behaviour in the classroom is demonstrated by Cooper *et al.* (1970).

Social reinforcement of teachers was also a factor in Barclay's (1970) study, in which the behaviour of school psychologists was successfully changed, resulting in a marked increase in the achievement of a group of mentally handicapped children with whose teachers the psychologists were working. Brown *et al.* (1969) demonstrated vividly in a case study using a multiple reversal design that changed teacher behaviour was highly contingent on continuing input of social reinforcement to the teacher by the trainer. Koenig (1967) has proposed that more tangible reinforcers be utilised to change teacher behaviour, but doubtless this would prove difficult to implement.

Other difficulties in implementing effective behaviour modification training in secondary schools are discussed by Macmillan and Kolvin (1977), who refer to the reluctance of some adults to use positive reinforcers. Poor motivation in teachers for after-school courses, differences in teachers' *ability* to change, difficulties in reshaping teacher behaviour after a very long and often over-learnt reinforcement history in non-compatible techniques, problems of discriminating the genuinely interested from the press-ganged, difficulties with teacher acceptance of responsibility for disturbed pupils, teacher reluctance to devote what they expect to be a disproportionate amount of time to a small number of pupils, even where this already occurs utilising other or no strategies, ethical objections to the use of extrinsic reinforcers, teacher anxiety about 'side effects' and whole classes demanding reinforcement (although there is no evidence that this has ever occurred), the inflexibility of secondary school organisations and the paucity of tangible reinforcers available for disruptive children within them, and so on, are mentioned.

Macmillan and Kolvin's (1977) own programme of training secondary-school teachers to use behaviour modification techniques is reported further in Kolvin *et al.* (1976) and Kolvin *et al.* (1981). Thirty-nine secondary-school teachers were trained by a psychologist to use behaviour modification techniques with a variety of problem behaviours demonstrated by 72 target children in 6 secondary schools. The children were aged 11-12 on entry to the programme, which lasted two terms. It is therefore not clear from these data whether similar effectiveness could be achieved with older disruptive pupils. The training procedure revolved around the provision of an introductory training manual followed by seminars, and (perhaps most importantly) by regular follow-up, support and consultation by the psychologist.

Kolvin *et al.* (1981) note that the early 'over-optimism' about behaviour modification has been tempered and the real difficulties facing behavioural applications in applied settings are being confronted. Many questions remain to be answered: How can change procedures be designed to provide the best opportunities for maintaining improvement and ensuring that it transfers across settings? Which types of behaviour are the most appropriate targets for intervention? What is the most effective way of teaching the application of behavioural techniques? How can continued application of techniques be ensured once training and back-up support cease? How can programmes be developed that fit readily into ordinary educational settings where the availability of manpower and support is minimal? How does a school's organisation and administration impinge on an intervention programme? The work of Kolvin *et al.* (1981) goes some small way towards answering these questions, and is a particularly recommended source.

Their programme utilised control and experimental groups of problem pupils, selected by (inevitably somewhat arbitrary) screening devices. It was felt that the introduction of tangible reinforcers was likely to present too many practical difficulties, in terms of clashes with the normal expectations and administrative exigencies of the day-to-day operation of the school, so much emphasis was given to the teachers'

use of 'social reinforcement' – the use of praise, disapproval and award-
ing or withholding of attention. (This study is thus, more specifically,
an evaluation of the effectiveness of this type of reinforcer with this
type of population, and of the effectiveness of Macmillan's training
and support procedures, rather than an evaluation of the practicability
and effectiveness of behaviour modification procedures in general, in
schools in general.)

While teachers may assume that social reinforcers have already, by
definition, failed with disruptive pupils, Kolvin *et al.* (1981) demonstrate by reference to the research evidence that this is not necessarily
so. Many studies have shown that while social *dis*approval is very frequent in teaching situations, *positive* social reinforcement is actually
far less frequently used than the teaching profession generally imagines.
The latter may therefore demonstrate effectiveness by virtue of its
scarcity value in what appear on the surface to be very improbable
situations. Nevertheless, it seems likely that behaviour modification
programmes with children older than the Kolvin *et al.* (1981) samples
may well need to include at some stage more tangible reinforcers than
the purely social. However, it can be argued that this should not be
countenanced until social reinforcement alone has been thoroughly
tried and demonstrated to be unsuccessful in isolation. Further, even in
instances where tangible reinforcements are eventually determined to
be necessary to effect behavioural change, they should always be paired
with social reinforcements to improve the child's responsiveness to the
latter. This will facilitate a process of 'weaning' a disruptive adolescent
off tangible reinforcers and on to purely social reinforcers at a later
date. In terms of the 'cascade' model (see Introduction), to maximise
cost-effectiveness the child should always be resourced only to the
degree necessary to maintain satisfactory behaviour. A child's response
to reinforcers should not be considered fixed for all time, and there are
dangers of reinforcement 'overkill' as well as the more obvious difficulty at times of finding any kind of reinforcer which is effective. As
the effectiveness of different types of reinforcers may vary for one child
from day to day, some sort of 'token' system with a range of reinforcers
available at fixed 'exchange rates' has major administrative advantages
and builds in to the programme an element of constant novelty, which
may be essential for success with some pupils. Two studies demonstrating the effective use of token procedures with secondary-age pupils are
cited by Kolvin *et al.* (1981). These authors also discuss at some length
the question of selection of target behaviours (referred to elsewhere
in this book), and cite several relevant studies on the modification of

academic behaviours. As we have seen, successful modification of academic behaviours also tends to result in lessening of disruptive behaviour,
whereas modification of disruptive behaviour does not necessarily result
in an automatic improvement in academic behaviour.

Notwithstanding these considerations and difficulties, the results of
the Kolvin *et al.* (1981) attempt to demonstrate effective training of
teachers in behaviour modification techniques in the natural environment are encouraging. The teachers in question were fairly experienced
and largely well-motivated. They were required to read the training
manual, and then attend three weekly one-hour small-group meetings
to discuss concepts and strategies, and experience a limited amount of
role-playing. Personal consultations between the psychologist and each
teacher followed, to elaborate the details of each programme. An average of nine personal consultations continued throughout the duration
of the programmes, allowing the psychologist to reinforce the efforts
of the teachers. By no means all the target behaviours were of a 'disruptive' nature — other, less obvious, problems were the focus of some
programmes. In a few cases where social reinforcement alone proved
ineffective, behavioural contracts giving access to a variety of concrete
rewards or preferred activities were introduced. A private 'points' system
recorded on a card kept by the pupil was utilised. The card also listed
desired and undesired behaviours and the positive or negative points
'value' attached to each. As the children improved, the targets were
made more difficult and tangible rewards became more distant until
they 'faded out' altogether. At the end of the consultation programme,
further written prescriptions for follow-up management were made
available to the schools. However, as the end of the programme co-
incided with the end of the academic year, follow-up was made very
difficult by the fact that the children changed to a different timetable,
very often with quite different teachers.

Changes in child behaviour were assessed via a rating scale completed
by the teachers: overall, 80 per cent of the children showed some
improvement in behaviour; 84 per cent showed improved academic
motivation; and 57 per cent improved academic attainment. However,
'disruptive' children tended to show less improvement than children
programmed with respect to other problems, and girls tended to improve more than boys. Those teachers who had had a higher number of
consultations tended to show greater improvements in behaviour (but
not academics) resulting from their programmes.

These data were supplemented by observations in the classroom
by an independent observer, in five of the six schools involved, of the

amount of 'on-task' behaviour from the subjects. Two observation periods during 'baseline', and six during programme, were carried out. The observational data indicated that significant improvement from baseline occurred early and late in the programmes, but not significantly so in the middle phase. Again, 'disruptive' children showed less improvement than children with other problems. There was some suggestion that boys showed significantly more on-task behaviour in the last phase of programming than girls, possibly implying some sex bias or 'halo effect' in the teacher ratings of girls. The focus on 'on-task' behaviour in the analysis of the observational data was perhaps a factor militating against a demonstration of the effectiveness of behaviour modification with 'disruptive children', since, as we have seen elsewhere, with such children, lessening disruptive behaviour does not necessarily increase 'on-task' behaviour.

The final form of assessment comprised the comparison of the experimental to the control group on a range of measures, including clinical assessment of psychiatric status, Devereux and Barker Lunn scaling, Rutter scale rating, personality testing and cognitive testing. For 'disruptive' children, the experimental group showed little change in comparison to controls by the mid-point of behaviour modification programming, but a substantial difference by the end of the 20-week programme. Positive results were also demonstrable at follow-up 2½ years later. Children with other problems undergoing modification showed significant improvement *vis-à-vis* controls at mid-point and at end of programming. These results seem to imply that behaviour modification procedures of the type used in this study take a while to 'bite' on disruptive children. Taking the Kolvin *et al.* (1981) results as a whole, considerable encouragement concerning the effectiveness of training ordinary schoolteachers in techniques of behaviour modification can be derived therefrom.

Spaulding and Showers (1974) report on a training exercise which used a melange of behaviour modification and a system of interaction analysis within a 'coping model' framework. Training proceeded via verbal input and discussion but also by observing a 'demonstration class' and video recordings, and by teachers analysing their own field observations. Student behaviour changes were observed by the experimenters, and while both experimental and control groups of children showed increased conforming behaviour, only the experimental group showed an increase in positive behaviours. Both experimental groups showed decreased aggression, while this increased in the control group. Training by an initial and then a follow-up course seemed as effective as the initial course followed by individual training, feedback and consultation by the experimenters. The amount of training time was substantial, and the theoretical framework somewhat complex. However, the former appears to have paid dividends, illustrating yet again that if a programme is worth doing, it is worth doing properly.

Summary

Small-group workshops for teachers to facilitate intra-school awareness and communication can have some positive effects. However, the vast majority of studies demonstrating teacher training to be effective in reducing disruptive behaviour in class are within a behaviour modification framework. There is no doubt that behaviour modification techniques can be effective in secondary schools, but effective behavioural INSET is easier to achieve in primary than secondary schools. However, substantial success has been demonstrated in secondary schools, and empirical guidelines for ensuring effectiveness and generalisation in time and space are increasingly found in the literature.

17 PUPIL TRAINING

Pupils who present disruptive behaviour may in many cases lack the personal and social skills to deal positively and effectively with social situations which they find stressful. In these cases, merely suppressing the disruptive behaviour is likely to result at best in short-term and situation-specific improvements. It is often argued that such children also, or alternatively, need to be taught pro-social skills, such as many ordinary children might learn at home. Almost all the widely varying schemes of this latter type could reasonably be grouped under the umbrella of 'social skills training', but as we shall see, this term is more commonly reserved for training programmes of a tightly structured behavioural type.

Burland *et al.* (1978) comment on a wide range of pupil training programmes for disruptive pupils. For instance, Meichenbaum (1973) has developed a number of techniques to modify what people say to themselves; these 'private monologues' being intended to produce positive rather than negative imagery. Some effectiveness is claimed in reducing impulsivity, anxiety and over-activity, but there is little evidence on effectiveness with disruptive adolescents. The same author is also responsible for a 'stress inoculation package' (Meichenbaum and Cameron, 1973) which utilises desensitisation and relaxation as the heart of a package of 'coping skills'. There is a growing literature on the use of relaxation techniques, hypnosis (including self-hypnosis) and biofeedback systems with children with various anxiety states, but the relevance of these techniques to disruptive adolescents seems somewhat marginal.

The aforementioned 'problem-solving strategies' of Lane (1978) and Stratford and Cameron (1979) can be taught to pupils (D'Zurilla and Goldfried, 1971), and there is some evidence that this can have an enduring impact on the behaviour of disruptive children (Spivack and Shure, 1974), who are given a framework for generating alternative (non-disruptive) problem solutions. Much informal counselling by teachers in school already features elements of this common-sense approach, but attention could usefully be paid to refining the process.

Robin (1976) combines training in problem-solving techniques with withdrawal and relaxation in his 'Turtle Technique'. Children who would usually respond with tantrums and aggression to failure and frustration are taught to withdraw 'into their shell' when under stress (curl up in a ball and close their eyes, if necessary), then relax all muscles, and while in the relaxed state, generate alternative (peaceful) solutions to the stress-inducing situation. Carrying out the Turtle Technique is certainly incompatible with being disruptive, and is a good example of what Hedderly (1978) has termed 'Orange-Juice Therapies' — 'therapies' which are effective by virtue of providing a displacement activity to divert the protagonists from what might otherwise be a self-reinforcing habitual conflict situation. This latter concept is a useful one for teachers to bear in mind — as much for use with their colleagues as with disruptive children.

A particularly interesting innovation is reported by Rose (1978), which serves to emphasise the reflexive nature of all social interventions. He began by teaching his small class of 11- to 14-year-olds with severe behaviour problems how to modify his (i.e. the teacher's) behaviour. The class agreed to attempt to modify the teacher's use of sarcasm (in a downward direction). They put the teacher on a token economy which offered the reinforcer 15 minutes' peace and quiet on Friday afternoon if the teacher's rate of emission of sarcastic behaviour was less than a pre-fixed criterion. The programme was successful. Convinced by the effectiveness and mutual benefit of behaviour modification techniques, the class then co-operated in devising a token system covering pupil behaviours. Schedules for token award and exchange for back-up reinforcers were worked out in detail. In this brief report, evaluation data are not as detailed and carefully controlled as one might wish, but there is evidence of greater group cohesion and improved standards in reading and some areas of arithmetic skills. Three individual pupils with problems of selfishness and verbal and physical aggression were more closely monitored and showed distinct improvement.

Burland *et al.* (1978) note other possible approaches, such as 'fixed-role therapy', 'rational-emotive therapy', 'personal effectiveness training', 'assertive training' and so forth, but there is little evidence of the effectiveness of these with disruptive adolescents.

Within secondary schools, attempts to improve children's personal development and social functioning are often brief and fragmentary, and most usually rely heavily on verbal input from the 'trainer'. Where 'Education for Personal Relationships' or 'Personal Development' courses form part of the curriculum, they are considered in Chapter 19, 'Curriculum'. DES (1978a) report on one such 'Personal Development Course' for a small section of a school population, occupying one lesson a week.

Purely verbal means of social skills training have proved singularly ineffective with disruptive pupils. Curtis and Gilmore (1981) report a 'group counselling' programme designed to 'sensitise' six secondary-school girls and make them more 'aware' of difficult social situations. Good group cohesion and relationships built up during the course, but at 12-week follow-up this had largely disappeared and no generalised results were evident. Giebink *et al.* (1968) utilised verbal means and a simulatory game situation in the attempt to teach adaptive responses to frustration to emotionally disturbed boys aged 10-12 years. Results were much more evident in the boys' verbal repertoires than in other kinds of behaviour, and there was little evidence of the subjects' changing their responses when outside of the experimental situation.

Miller *et al.* (1968) reported on a three-year elementary school programme which combined verbal input with role-playing. Compared to control groups, the children showed improved interpersonal relationships, personal effectiveness and problem-solving, although there was no carry-over into academic achievement. Whether similar techniques would be effective with adolescents, particularly if not preselected for such a programme, is not clear. There is certainly some evidence that purely verbal means such as counselling can improve academic attainment (Mezzano, 1968; and Baymur and Patterson, 1960), but demonstrating behavioural gains by such means has proved much more difficult. Henry and Killman (1979) review studies which have evaluated the effectiveness of group counselling in secondary-school settings. They note that subjects who volunteered for the experience showed greater gains than subjects who were coerced into attendance. Furthermore, behavioural and directive groups achieved greater success than client-centred or non-directive groups. The time spent in the groups focusing on the aims and objectives of the programme was an important factor in success or otherwise.

An exception to this trend is reported by Kolvin *et al.* (1981), who deployed six well-qualified and supported social workers in secondary schools in the North-east of England to operate a system of 'discussion groups' along non-directive, Rogerian 'group-therapy' lines for 60 pupils with a wide range of difficulties. Not all the pupils could be characterised as 'disruptive' in the anti-social sense. The group therapy programme ran for just three months (one term). At follow-up immediately the programme ended, few differences were apparent. However, at follow-up three years later, the children presented as less socially isolated, parents reported improved adjustment and behaviour at home, and teacher reports on the Rutter scale showed significant improvement on both 'neurotic' and 'anti-social' aspects. At medium-term follow-up, the children's educational attainment as well as their adjustment had improved, but by final follow-up at three years the gains in attainment had 'washed out'. There was some evidence that adjustment gains for 'neurotic' type children were more durable at three-year follow-up than adjustment gains for 'anti-social' type children. To the researchers' surprise, they found no evidence that the cohesiveness and openness of the group was related to outcome measures. It is noted that the programme's cost-effectiveness was actually less than might be imagined, since high training and support costs for the 'therapists' had to be included in such calculations. However, the results are clearly encouraging, and represent a significant departure from other research findings.

Kolvin *et al.* (1981) explain the 'less-than-exciting' evaluation results of other studies in terms of those authors having looked 'for the wrong thing, at the wrong time, in studies often on far too small a scale'. In particular, measures of academic attainment and social isolation had been shown to be far less sensitive indices of the effects of this kind of intervention than were teacher-, parent- and self-reports. Further, changes might only appear some considerable time after completion of the intervention, and few studies had included follow-up at sufficiently long a term to 'capture' this effect. It may well be, of course, that a teacher faced with the problem of a disruptive child in the classroom would wish for an intervention which had immediate effects rather than effects three years later. However, for those interested in this area, the Kolvin *et al.* (1981) results certainly provide encouragement, and their book also contains a useful review of a great many studies on the effectiveness of group counselling of various sorts, with various age groups, directed at various target problems.

Turning now to the more structured schemes with more diverse training techniques which have labelled themselves 'Social Skills Training', we find that successful outcomes are still by no means automatic. Sarason and Sarason (1974) provide a useful manual on social skills training techniques for teachers. Marzillier (1978) provides a methodical review of some of the better designed studies of 'improving social behaviour by means of demonstration, practice, guidance and feedback'. However, the review shows that with a wide variety of target groups, generalisation and durability of behavioural gains have been demonstrated in a minority of studies.

Chandler (1973) used video feedback to develop interpersonal perception and role-taking skills during a 10-week summer programme for 45 chronically delinquent 11- to 13-year-old boys. 'Experimental' subjects showed greater post-programme gains on a projective 'social egocentrism scale' than controls did. More to the point, although the causative links are obscure, is the fact that controls had acquired significantly more convictions at 18 months follow-up than had 'experimental' children.

Another device for ensuring feedback other than the purely verbal was utilised by Minuchin *et al.* (1967), who had children observe each other through a one-way mirror during role-play sessions. The children rated each other's performance, and cash rewards were available for the children with the highest ratings. The 10-session programme with six aggressive and anti-social children from a residential unit focused on trouble-avoiding classroom skills like staying on-task, taking turns, sharing, conversation skills, etc. Few evaluative details of any clarity are noted, but it seems that by the end of the programme children showed better attention spans and self-organisational ability, although there is no evidence concerning duration or generalisation of these gains.

Goldstein *et al.* (1980) point out that the search for one technique to cure all social ills is naive in the extreme and suggest that research should be largely concerned with determining which techniques work with which types and groups of problem children. Their own social skills training programme, termed 'Structured Learning' (of pro-social skills), consists of (1) modelling, (2) role-playing, (3) performance feedback, and (4) transfer of training. The approach is well structured and clearly and tightly delineated. An annotated bibliography of research reports on the approach is provided, with many successful outcomes reported, but only a few studies pertain to disruptive adolescents.

One report describes the training of children in 'empathising' in conflict situations, but no generalisation outside the training situation was achieved. Another reports similar results with attempts to train 'negotiation skills', but notes the interesting finding that peers proved as good trainers as adults (cf. Chapter 13). A third study attempting to train 'self-control' by structured learning also failed to achieve skill transfer. However, a programme to train 'resistance reducing behaviour and negotiation skills' found discrimination training and structured learning equally effective and did produce generalisation. Another on 'helping others' showed good skill acquisition and generalisation. A programme to train for 'assertiveness' found structured learning in groups more effective than the same technique on an individual basis, but generalisation was achieved in both cases. Although only half these studies have demonstrated generalisation, Goldstein *et al.*'s book is a model of a well-thought-through programme.

Social skills training within a more heavily behavioural framework has tended to show better outcomes. In these cases, specific verbal behaviours in interactions with others are precisely defined and trained towards by a process of instructing, modelling, prompting, role-playing, shaping, feedback and reinforcement. Such detailed approaches have proved effective in teaching conversation skills to delinquent girls (Minkin *et al.*, 1976); posture and gesture skills to delinquent girls (Maloney *et al.*, 1976); and smiling, sharing, touching and compliment-ing skills to elementary-school children (Cooke and Apolloni, 1976). Cooke and Apolloni demonstrated not only generalisation over time but also transfer of skills to untrained children coming into contact with trained subjects.

Werner *et al.* (1975) devised a training programme to prepare delin-quent youths for encounters with the police in a programme known as 'What Do You Say to a Cop?' Specific behaviours which would elicit a favourable outcome were trained towards (e.g. lowered gaze, politeness and briefness of answers to questions, modes of expression of under-standing, concern, co-operation and intent to reform). The training procedure proved highly effective and resulted in much more positive ratings by community policemen, but no data are available on long-term effects on conviction rates. Clearly, programmes of this kind can be construed as training children to manipulate adults (skills which many middle-class children acquire more naturally), skills which pre-sumably need not necessarily be used by the child for the objectives which the trainer had in mind. There are descriptions in the literature of successful training of children in techniques of altering the behaviour of their peers and their teachers towards them, although no evidence of long-term effectiveness and generalisation with disruptive adolescents has emerged from the literature search. While teachers might consider the former acceptable, few would probably venture into the latter area, but this would not preclude such training being carried out by an extra-school agency.

Closely related to social skills training by behavioural methods are systems of self-recording and self-reinforcement, which are an exten-sion of behaviour modification techniques. These can be targeted on any behaviour according to the needs of the situation, and have the advantage of requiring a much more modest time input from a super-vising adult than fully-fledged social skills training.

Many secondary schools utilise 'report card' systems, whereby dis-ruptive pupils collect the signatures and comments of each classteacher on the card during the day. The card is checked by a senior teacher at intervals. Extensions of the scheme may include having the card taken home and signed by parents before being returned, and parents may be asked to apply domestic rewards and punishments on the basis of the report. This latter can also apply in school on a contingency contracting basis, and is facilitated if a framework of rating or token/point award is inbuilt, as nebulous comments from teachers result in inconsistent application of the scheme.

Self-recording by pupils is often useful as a follow-on from a brief period 'on report', or for some pupils self-recording gives an alternative to be tried before placing a child 'on report'. If self-recording by itself proves insufficient, it can be linked with self-reinforcement to provide another alternative strategy to the 'report' system.

Lovitt (1973) reports on seven 'self-management projects with children with behavioural disabilities'. Unfortunately all these are single case studies except for the last, which details the progress of nine 7-year-old behaviourally disordered boys in 'correcting, counting, timing, charting and evaluating' their performance on academic tasks. The system was more complex than many precision teaching schemes (? precision learning), but the 7-year-olds seemed to cope admirably with it, and were capable of using the system effectively in a variety of different classroom environments. Perhaps the children were too busy charting to get into mischief, but this is no denial of the effectiveness of the approach.

The much-quoted study of Broden *et al.* (1971) demonstrated the effectiveness of similar but less complex self-recording techniques with two inattentive 14-year-old pupils. Dramatic results were achieved in increasing study behaviour and reducing disruptive behaviour by self-recording alone, the addition of social reinforcement resulting in only a slight further gain. Long-term follow-up results are not available, but there seems little reason why the pupil should not continue using the system for as long as the need is felt. Gallagher (1972) used a more highly structured self-recording scheme involving timers in a residential special school with 16 boys aged 8-11 years, and reported improved attention to task and academic achievement.

In the UK, literature on self-recording in secondary schools is associated with the name of McNamara (1979), who notes the effectiveness of the technique with adults with dieting, smoking, study and psychiatric problems. McNamara and Heard (1976) describe the successful use of self-recording with a whole class of difficult girls. It was found that the children did record accurately, and study behaviour increased while disruption reduced. McNamara (1979) documents a study which demonstrated the effectiveness of self-recording in two out of three classes in a comprehensive school. Both these papers are commended to teachers as practical and simple expositions of methods of procedure.

A step on from self-recording is the addition of self-reinforcement. Lovitt and Curtiss (1969), Glynn (1970), Bolstad and Johnson (1972), Kaufman and O'Leary (1972) and Felixbrod and O'Leary (1973) all found self-reinforcement effective in modifying classroom behaviour. Glynn (1970) and Felixbrod and O'Leary (1973) found self-reinforcement just as effective as teacher reinforcement, while Lovitt and Curtiss (1969) found self-reinforcement *more* effective than teacher reinforcement, noting that the *amount* of self-prescribed reinforcement did not appear to be the determining variable.

Drabman *et al.* (1973) studied the effects of self-reinforcement on the behaviour and work-rate of eight 9- to 10-year-old boys with adjustment problems in an after-school remedial class. An initial programme of teacher-awarded token reinforcement was faded into child-monitored self-recording and self-reinforcement, with checking by adults being phased out intermittently in four stages. Behaviour gains were maintained and the children gained an average of 0.75 years of reading age in 2½ months. There was no automatic generalisation outside of this class, but that would not necessarily be expected in this case.

Although few of the studies of self-reinforcement have concerned themselves with disruptive adolescents in secondary schools, the techniques of self-recording and self-reinforcement would seem promising. Macmillan and Morrison (1979) state 'an evaluation of the studies indicates that when compared to externally imposed change, self-regulation strategies tend to be equally efficacious in the control of behaviour. However, self-control techniques are more successful if some form of external control training precedes or accompanies them.' McLaughlin (1976), after reviewing the state of the field, commented: 'self-regulation strategies seem to be as efficacious in the control of behaviour as strategies that involve externally imposed change'.

Summary

Purely verbal means of teaching children pro-social skills on the whole show limited effectiveness with disruptive adolescents, although some benefits may accrue with other groups. One UK study reports positive long-term effects of non-directive Rogerian group counselling with young adolescents emanating a range of problem behaviours, but less significant short-term effects. More detailed and intensive social skills training programmes utilising modelling, role-playing and personal or video feedback have produced better effects, particularly where reinforcement has been utilised within a behavioural framework. However, generalisation and long-term duration do not occur automatically, and successes on these criteria are reported by only half the studies. Systems of self-recording and self-reinforcement have the advantage of requiring less teacher time, and the evidence on self-recording, in particular, suggests that it could provide a most useful adjunct to existing measures. Self-reinforcement may well be as effective as teacher reinforcement, but is likely to prove more difficult than self-recording to mesh with existing school practices. To what extent any of these procedures would be effective with the most disruptive of adolescents, who were highly motivated to be disruptive, is not clear.

18 PARENT TRAINING

Many programmes for disruptive pupils refer to 'work with parents' in some form or another as being integral to their approach. In many cases, however, this liaison with parents often appears to lack any specific theoretical, empirical or even purposive structure.

Hewett and Blake (1973) refer to several studies dating back to 1960 which involved parents in total educational programmes for 'disturbed' pupils, but note that little evidence of effectiveness is cited. Some researchers reported strong resistance to getting involved in such programmes on the part of parents, who seemed to prefer to deny the existence of the child's problems. Yet many teachers of disruptive pupils felt that 'lack of parental co-operation' was a major factor in limiting the effectiveness of educational efforts, and work with parents clearly represents an important area of endeavour.

Some success has been achieved. D'Angelo and Walsh (1967) compared the effectiveness of four patterns of intervention: treatment for the child alone, group therapy for the parents alone, a combination of both, and a control group. Child treatment alone or in combination with parent treatment yielded results worse than untreated controls, while group therapy for parents alone appeared to result in some improvement in the children's behaviour. Lisle (1968) found no difference in pupil adjustment among a variety of counselling approaches involving children, parents, teachers or some combination of the three. However, treatment approaches *without* pupil involvement were found to be more effective for improving *teacher-perceived* pupil adjustment. Glavin and Quay (1969) reported a similar study to that of D'Angelo and Walsh (1967), and concluded that interventions with disturbed children are probably more effective if they involve the parents rather than the child.

However, none of these studies pertained to secondary-school children, and the forms of 'therapy' used were not always clear. In the UK, Kolvin *et al.* (1976) evaluated a combined parent and teacher consultation programme operated by social workers, aimed at disruptive adolescents. Results do not appear to be very encouraging (Kolvin *et al.*, 1981).

More substantial and encouraging evidence comes from studies based on behavioural methodology. Johnson and Katz (1973) reviewed many studies which had successfully demonstrated that parents could be trained to modify their children's behaviour. Most of the behaviour change achieved by these studies was within the home environment, however. Nevertheless, the work of Tharp and Wetzel (1969) demonstrated that parents could achieve great control over their children's behaviour even when the children were out of immediate supervision in community settings. Rinn (1975) reported on a programme of training parents of disruptive children in groups. The children were up to 18 years old, but the mean age was 9. Both of a child's parents were required to attend the course, and pay a $30 tuition fee, of which $10 was refunded if they attended regularly and implemented the strategies described. By the last session of the course, only 5 per cent of the parents failed to report improvement in their children, and at follow-up 6-18 months later only 15 per cent reported lack of continued improvement. Although queries are raised by the effect of sample attrition and by the variability and method of follow-up, this study appears to demonstrate effectiveness well above spontaneous remission rate with minimal time investment and at extremely low cost to the taxpayer.

Of more immediate relevance to teachers may be the various behavioural systems of linking home and school. Many schools have difficulty finding anything by way of rewards and/or punishments which affect the behaviour of disruptive adolescents in school. However, such reinforcers may exist at home, and a system of recording the child's behaviour at school and reporting this to the parents, who apply reinforcers as appropriate, may serve to get round this difficulty with minimal time investment by the school. McKenzie *et al.* (1968) report significant improvements in the academic work output of learning disabled children by the implementation of such a scheme, whereby daily feedback to parents resulted in variations in pocket money made available. Hall *et al.* (1970) and Schumaker *et al.* (1977) both report effective use of this method to improve the behaviour and classroom performance of disruptive adolescents aged up to 19 years.

Summary

Many educational programmes for disruptive pupils have referred to parental involvement, but this has rarely had a specific purposive structure. However, there is some evidence that intensive work with parents is more effective in producing child improvements than is work directly with the children, and this is obviously an important, if rather neglected, area. Behavioural methodology has proved particularly effective in parent training. Behavioural systems of home-school liaison have proved effective in reducing the disruptive behaviour in school of adolescents up to 19 years of age, with little time investment from the school.

Part Six

IN-SCHOOL ORGANISATIONAL FACTORS
AND THE CONTINUUM MODEL

19 CURRICULUM

As noted in the Preface, this chapter does not purport to review fully all the literature on the relationship of curriculum to disruptiveness, and the topic has already been referred to in a section ('Behavioural versus Academic Objectives') of the Introduction to this book.

There is substantial evidence that learning difficulties are frequently found in children with behavioural difficulties, and it is generally accepted that the former may cause the latter just as frequently as vice versa. Thus schools with under-resourced remedial departments, or who try to impose a highly academic curriculum on children from homes that place more value on practical skills, can expect a higher than average incidence of behavioural problems, other things being equal. However, a pre-existing, adequately resourced, well-balanced and appropriate curriculum will be assumed in discussion of the following studies, which largely refer to the effectiveness of additions to such a curriculum. It goes without saying that attempts to deal with behaviour problems resulting from massive dysjunction in the curriculum by throwing in a mini-course on pupil self-management are unlikely to meet with much success. Further, as Docking (1980) points out, curriculum content has to be determined on grounds of educational value rather than on just whether reductions in disruptive behaviour result therefrom. No doubt high pupil interest and involvement might be gained from lessons in guerrilla warfare and safe-cracking, but few teachers would consider that an adequate reason to adopt such an approach. Docking further points out that disruptive behaviour may not result so much from what is taught, but from the way it is taught.

An interesting attempt to provide a curriculum for children with difficulties in school is described by Chard (1980) and Rendell (1980), whose Individual Studies Department operates not by the espousal of a particular curriculum structure which is believed to be generally 'therapeutic', but by offering the flexibility in individual curriculum programming that many secondary schools find so difficult to achieve. The Department provides the security of a fixed base, relationships with fewer and more pastorally oriented teachers, regular attention to basic skills, the opportunity to take CSE (Certificate of Secondary Education) examinations in 13 subjects, work experience and a wide range of non-academic, community-oriented activities which are available once the day's academic targets have been met. The Department has been found helpful with low-ability, low-motivation and disruptive children. Although it is noted that disruptive behaviour and absenteeism have decreased very substantially, this may be due to factors in addition to the establishment of the Department, and no harder evaluative data are available. However, teachers will find Rendell's paper very interesting.

Webb and Cormier (1972), in an intervention of greater specificity and smaller scale, withdrew 22 disruptive junior high students from maths classes and gave them a specific academic programme where all teaching was geared to specific behavioural objectives, and students were rewarded with free time when their daily assignments were completed. Increased task-related behaviour and reduced disruptive behaviour resulted, and this effect was maintained when the students returned to ordinary classes. However, that success is not automatic was demonstrated by Ahlstrom and Havighurst (1971), whose 400 socially maladapted urban boys were divided into two groups, one to follow an ordinary classroom programme and one to follow a modified curriculum involving work experience. Both groups were monitored for six years, but the 'experimental' group did not make any better subsequent adjustment to working life. However, this latter is a very stringent criterion, and most studies of disruptive behaviour in school have been content to evaluate in terms of improved behaviour within that specific environment.

Other researchers have looked at the effectiveness of more restricted and specific curricular inputs which had the intention of reducing disruptiveness. Garibaldi (1979) describes School Survival Courses integrated with the timetable which give the children strategies for becoming better learners, techniques for staying out of trouble, and practice in gaining insight into the consequences of the behaviour of themselves and others. One high school offers a mini-course for pupils on dealing with assaults and disruptive behaviour, which includes definitions of deviance, explication of the range of consequences for misdeeds, and suggested steps for reporting attacks and assaults.

Few studies detailing the teaching of behavioural methods to pupils as part of the regular curriculum came to light. Perhaps behavioural techniques are considered too powerful to be made generally available to children. The major exception is the study of Lovitt (1973), who describes the teaching of self-management skills as part of the curriculum. (Chapter 13 on volunteers and Chapter 17 on pupil training describe the teaching of behavioural skills to individual pupils on an *ad hoc* basis.) Lovitt had his 'behavioural disability' students taught to do their own scheduling and programming, take responsibility for assignment completion, evaluate their own work, plot their own progress and set their own contingencies and rewards. This had the advantage of taking a substantial organisational burden off the classteacher and the children were well motivated by the scheme. However, evaluation results are bitty.

Other curricular inputs can be more sweeping and less immediately pragmatic. The DES (1978a) mention a 'personal development course', and 'education for personal relationships' and 'social education' seem to be growth areas in schools, as is 'health education'. Ojemann's (1967) review paper is cited as something of a classic in this area. Rather than have pupils go through 'group awareness exercises', Ojemann preferred the specific teaching of psychological concepts via discussion of example scenarios. He cites observational evidence from ordinary lessons (albeit on rather obscure dimensions) that his experimental groups became less extra-punitive and judgemental as a result of understanding more about human motivation and behaviour. Trained groups have demonstrated greater understanding of human behaviour on post-course tests than non-trained groups, and there is some evidence that 'insecure and unstable' children can benefit quite as much as their better adjusted comrades. Many of the studies cited by Ojemann have unfortunately relied on paper-and-pencil tests, but the results of those that have not are encouraging, although there is no suggestion that such techniques are particularly effective with disruptive children. This also applies to the studies of Sprinthall (1974) and Long (1970, 1974).

In the UK, Manchester Education Committee (1974) describe a Social Education Project with an emphasis on group awareness and group work method. The intention seems to be to help pupils develop insights into, and involvement with, various aspects of society, but 'the method of work takes precedence over the content'. Unfortunately the 'evaluation' section of the report is disappointing.

The overall results from these curriculum innovations are thus not particularly solid or encouraging, but curriculum specialists would doubtless argue that where such projects are tailored for a wide cross-section of the school, it would be unrealistic to expect a specific and lasting effect on that small proportion of pupils who are consistently disruptive. There is, of course, the contrary view that the surest way to kill children's interest in something is to include it in the curriculum.

Summary

In addition to the body of general aetiological evidence which suggests that failure to cater for learning difficulties can result in disruptive behaviour, there is some evidence that where a school is able to be highly flexible in devising individual curricula for disruptive pupils, disruption and absenteeism are reduced. Giving pupils specific work targets and free time on target achievement has reduced disruptiveness in adolescents. Teaching children psychological concepts can produce more understanding and tolerance of the behaviour of others, but effects on disruption remain unevaluated. The work in this area is full of interesting ideas but limited in hard evaluative data.

20 ROUTINE SANCTIONS

In the 'best-practice' sample of schools visited, the DES (1978a) noted that all sanctions were traditional. In the main they appeared to depend for their effect on the respect of the pupil for the teacher administering punishment, on their irksomeness to the pupil, or on an appeal to communal responsibility. A 'dressing-down' could still be effective, if the pupil respected the teacher. Referral to a senior teacher might lead to various courses of action, such as exclusion from a frequently disrupted class or part of the timetable, with work set and done under the supervision of senior staff. General misbehaviour or absenteeism might be met by being 'put on report', involving every lesson teacher's signature or comments being shown to a senior teacher at regular intervals.

Such treatment was felt to be irksome for many pupils, but effective only for some. Some children *liked* being on report as it provided security and attention from teachers. In some schools recalcitrant pupils were attached to senior staff and had to follow them throughout the day. This too proved agreeable to some pupils. Detention also had its hazards, in that transport home could prove very difficult, and this caused some anxiety, particularly in the case of girls during the winter months.

Maughan and Ouston (1979) noted from their more detailed research that levels of punishment varied considerably between schools, but seemed to have little bearing — either positively or negatively — on outcomes for the children. Two exceptions were unofficial physical punishment and very frequent tellings-off in lessons, which were actually associated with *worse* behaviour. By contrast, all kinds of rewards, from praise in lessons to more public commendations or formal reward systems, did seem to result in better outcomes. The overall picture for rewards 'provided a sharp contrast with the results on punishment'. The more immediate forms of positive feedback showed the strongest association with good outcome. Maughan and Ouston (1979) comment: 'the contrast became even more striking when we found that in all schools punishments tended to be more frequent than praise — in the ratio of two or three to one'.

Rutter *et al.* (1979) noted that where a 'disciplinary' as distinct from a 'welfare' attitude to pupils was adopted by teachers, better behaviour resulted, but that schools where a lot of punishment was *used* enjoyed no better behaviour than schools where little was used. The consistent setting of widely known standards of behaviour resulted in better behaviour, but high levels of corporal punishment (official or unofficial) were strongly associated with worse behaviour.

It is clear that what is prescribed as punishment may often prove not to be punishing. Madsen *et al.* (1968) demonstrated experimentally that the more teachers said 'sit down', the more children stood up. Thomas *et al.* (1968) demonstrated that systematic variation of the teacher's classroom behaviour directly affected the amount of disruption, and that increases in 'punishment' could actually produce increased disruption. Nor are rewards free from unexpected effects. McCullough (1972) showed that praise can be punishing to some older pupils if delivered too publicly.

The most frequently used 'punishment' is undoubtedly the verbal reprimand. McAllister *et al.* (1969) present one of the few studies demonstrating that verbal reprimand can work at all. In this case it was coupled with praise for the whole group when everyone was behaving well. The reprimands were very brief, directive and stern and included the pupil's name. In a class of 25 16- to 19-year-olds, disruption was reduced and study behaviour increased by this method.

However, Rutter *et al.* (1979) report that *frequent* reprimands alone by teachers result in worse behaviour. O'Leary *et al.* (1970) noted that with elementary children, quiet reprimands were usually more effective in reducing disruptive behaviour than loud reprimands. Kazdin and Klock (1973) draw attention to the non-verbal component of reprimands and praise, and in their study they found that non-verbal expressions of approval from the teacher (smiles, nods, gestures, etc.) were effective on their own in improving student attention.

Turning to another time-hallowed favourite, 'detention', it is noteworthy that Rutter *et al.* (1979) found no association between the use of detention and behavioural outcomes (i.e. it made no difference). The same applied to giving 'lines' or extra work impositions. Docking (1980) gives a useful discussion of the practical problems inherent in the use of detention, not the least being that if children are given extra academic work as a punishment, this is unlikely to improve their attitude to such work at other times, while penalties unrelated to the offence are likely to be resented. Hall *et al.* (1971) report on various studies which have utilised carefully structured 'detention' schemes, to good effect. A study with 16-year-olds where low marks in lessons resulted in extra *tuition* after school to remedy the difficulty led to much higher marks being achieved in normal lessons. In another study, ten children in a special class for disruptive children received five minutes' detention for every out-of-seat behaviour. This dramatically reduced the incidence of this behaviour. Unfortunately in both studies the experimental period was short, and to what extent the effectiveness of the punishments was due to their novelty value is not clear.

The third punishment in the traditional 'trinity' is, of course, corporal punishment. We have already noted that Rutter *et al.* (1979) found high levels of corporal punishment (official or unofficial) associated with *worse* behaviour. Clegg (1962) and Reynolds and Murgatroyd (1977) present evidence which supports this finding. Many schools claim that corporal punishment is hardly ever used, but in the National Children's Bureau Study of a large sample of children born in 1958, it was found that 80 per cent of the 16-year-olds were in secondary schools where corporal punishment was still used (1977). Musgrave (1977) found no evidence from examination of punishment books that the use of corporal punishment in elementary schools had fallen between 1900 and 1939. A survey by the Inner London Education Authority (1978a) in 1978 found little evidence of change in the incidence of corporal punishment over the previous three years, and a substantial minority of schools resorted to this measure frequently. ILEA has since, of course, abolished the practice.

The DES (1978a) noted that schools were inconsistent in their use of corporal punishment even within themselves, citing one school where one 'house' used the cane three times more frequently than another of the same size. The DES further comment: 'some schools reported that many children were so accustomed to severe beatings at home that they were impervious to corporal punishment at school, and indeed, that some children claimed to prefer it to other more inconvenient punishments'. This is supported by the work of Sallows (1972), who studied a sample of normal and a sample of deviant children at home, and reported that while the normal sample's parents used almost entirely verbal punishment, the deviant sample's parents used a substantial amount of physical punishment — with less effect.

The British Psychological Society (1980) reviewed all the available evidence on the effectiveness of corporal punishment, and concluded: 'We can find no evidence which shows that corporal punishment is of value in classroom management. We have found evidence of its disadvantages, although such evidence is not of the highest scientific rigour.' This report also notes that children often express a preference for corporal punishment. The BPS note that 'the use of C.P. in schools has long since been officially abandoned in the majority of Western European countries as well as throughout the communist bloc', and that nearly all the professional organisations concerned with the welfare of children favour the abolition of corporal punishment. The report comments: 'in order that physical punishment may be optimally effective a number of conditions have to be observed that cannot obtain in a normal school setting'.

The BPS report that there is evidence that where corporal punishment has been abandoned, an improvement in behaviour is often reported, and this is supported by Munro's (1981) account of recent research in Scotland. No school which had abolished corporal punishment had considered reintroducing it.

The amount of research evidence against the practice of corporal punishment is vast. STOPP (1979) publish a reading list of 225 items in support of abolition, of which many are solid, reliable, respectable objective research studies, in sharp contrast to the subjectivism which tends to characterise the retentionists.

The view that, even if corporal punishment is ineffective with frequent offenders, it serves to deter others, is frequently put forward, and there is some research evidence to support this view. Walters *et al.* (1965) found that where children observed a peer punished for a misbehaviour, the probability of the observers' omitting those behaviours was reduced. There is no evidence as to the duration of this effect. However, many people might find the prospect of public flogging purely 'pour encourager les autres' not particularly acceptable, particularly if they were parents themselves.

A fourth type of sanction is 'deprivation of privileges'. That this is less frequent in usage may be suggestive that school children enjoy few privileges of which they can be deprived. The method of time-out described in Chapter 9 can of course be construed as deprivation of the privilege of remaining in the classroom. Clarizio (1976) has reviewed research in the area of privilege deprivation. It is clear, though perhaps not immediately obvious, that the effectiveness of this form of punishment will depend on how much the pupil values what he or she is threatened with losing, *and* on how clearly the way to regain the privileges is shown.

Many studies of deprivation of privileges have been conducted within a behaviourist framework, where the system is usually referred to as 'response cost'. The behaviour resulting in loss of reward, the reward lost, and the means of regaining the reward are carefully specified *in advance*. This enables extremely consistent application of the system. Provided it is well structured, the scheme can be effective, but you do have to have something you can lose. The previously cited studies of Hall *et al.* (1971) could also be construed as 'response cost' systems. Broden *et al.* (1970a) found a system of 'minus' points accumulating to an after-school detention (which could be 'bought off' by plus points gained by good behaviour), effective with 13- to 15-year-olds.

Many sanctions in secondary schools have been in use so long that they have entered into the folk rituals of the teaching profession. There is substantial evidence that the children's perceptions of the effectiveness of various sanctions is considerably at variance with the teachers' perceptions, yet many teachers proceed on the assumption that 'teacher knows best'. Burns (1978) asked 785 11- to 15-year-olds and their teachers to rank 12 rewards in terms of preference and believed effectiveness. The teachers thought praise from themselves was the most powerful reward, but the children were lukewarm about this. Within school, the children thought receiving prizes would be a powerful incentive, although the best thing would be a favourable report home. The teachers were indifferent re these latter.

The references to prizes must be qualified by the findings of Rutter *et al.* (1979), who found good behaviour associated quite strongly with public praise, but not with the award of prizes, although *academic* improvement was associated with the latter. However, we have already referred to the need to make a careful distinction between public and private praise for some pupils. Indeed, Burns (1978) found that boys valued private praise more highly than girls, and this doubtless relates to Davie's (1972) finding that girls are more anxious for parental approval, boys for peer approval.

The high effectiveness reported by pupils for good or bad reports home is confirmed by the studies of Davies and Thorne (1977) and Highfield and Pinsent (1972). Of course it may be argued that disruptive pupils frequently have unco-operative or anti-school parents whose response to such reports is unlikely to be helpful, but this is an empirical question on which no specific data seem to be available. Davies and Thorne also found that children regarded the rewards of 'time off lessons' and 'extra time at favoured lessons' as highly desirable; much more desirable than teacher praise. Again, pupils became more ambivalent to public praise the older they were. The most effective punishments were considered to be 'a letter home about bad behaviour' and 'parents asked to come to school'. Older pupils were generally more sceptical about the effectiveness of punishments than younger pupils, and were particularly unimpressed by 'extra work' and 'detention'. On the whole, rewards were endorsed as effective much more strongly than punishments, and the involvement of parents in both received strong support.

In the Davies and Thorne (1977) study, corporal punishment was considered quite effective, although not as effective as home contact. Munro (1981) reports that in Scotland pupils are divided on the effectiveness of the belt, but there is a clearer consensus on the effectiveness of parental involvement. Scottish children also seem to find detention more effective than English children.

A more subtle enquiry has been conducted by O'Hagan and Edmunds (1983), who explored pupils' perceptions of different teacher styles of response to disruptive behaviour. A total of 120 13- and 14-year-old pupils were asked to rate six teacher control 'styles' along six evaluative dimensions. The six styles were: 'reactive hostile' (teacher only punishes when the class are not behaving properly); 'initiatory instrumental' (teacher punishes occasionally at random to demonstrate purposefulness in maintaining peace and quiet); 'pro-social' (teacher punishes a pupil for being unpleasant to a peer); 'initiatory hostile' (teacher picks on and punishes pupils for selfish pleasure); 'reactive instrumental' (teacher reluctant to punish and only does it when the class misbehave), and 'non-aggression' (teacher never punishes irrespective of class behaviour).

The pupils felt that the 'pro-social' style was the most justifiable, followed by the 'reactive instrumental' style. They had little time for the totally non-aggressive style. The 'initiatory hostile' style was felt likely to be the most effective form of containing disruptive behaviour, but it was also felt likely to result in a lot of truancy from such lessons. The 'reactive instrumental' style was felt likely to result in maximum pupil application to work, good behaviour from the class as a whole and low truancy rates. Interesting interaction effects according to sex of pupil and teacher are reported. O'Hagan and Edmunds conclude that 'apparently successful attempts to control disruptive conduct by intimidatory practice may have deleterious consequences in other ways'. Neither person nor situation variance predominated in the results, and it is noted that this suggests that in the ordinary school it is as important to be aware of potentially disturbing situations as it is to be of potentially disruptive pupils.

There is a great deal of research literature on the effectiveness of punishment which is not necessarily related to the school environment. Reviews of this are provided by Church (1963), Solomon (1964), Azrin and Holz (1966), and Mayer *et al.* (1968). Wright (1973) presents an overview directly related to schools. From these and other reviews referred to below, guidelines on how to use punishment effectively may be drawn. However, as the BPS (1980) has already pointed out, the requisite conditions for effective use may not always pertain in schools – in these circumstances, teachers would need to demonstrate professionalism and not carry on punishing for want of consideration of alternatives.

Various interesting pointers emerge from the more academic research. Rotter (1966) reviewed a number of studies and found that 'rewards' and the experience of success were not always reinforcing. There was evidence that the extent to which a child saw these as reinforcing depended on whether the child saw the rewards or success as achieved by his own skill and effort rather than sheer luck or chance. This would seem to imply that providing pleasant experiences for disruptive pupils might make them happier, but is not likely to make them better behaved, unless the pleasant experiences are made contingent upon good behaviour.

Parke (1969) studied the effectiveness of various punishment conditions on 6- and 7-year-old boys. There were variations in timing of punishment, intensity of punishment, relationship between agent and recipient of punishment, and amount of rationale given for punishment. Parke found that the provision of 'high cognitive structure' (rationale and explanation of offence and punishment) was effective, and that it modified the operation of the other factors. High-intensity punishment was more effective than low-intensity when no 'cognitive structure' was given, but not when 'cognitive structure' was given. Similarly, early punishment was more effective than late punishment under low cognitive structure, but not under high cognitive structure, under low- but not high-intensity punishment, and under good relationship but not weak relationship conditions. Finally, children with prior good relationships with the punisher were more resistant to deviation than children where this did not apply, but only under low cognitive structure conditions.

To summarise:

Rationalisation/explanation/clarification is effective.
Rationale and mild sanction has same effect as severe sanction.
Early sanction without rationale = late sanction with rationale.
Early better than late for mild sanctions.
Early better than late where relationships good.

Unfortunately, for our purposes, Parke's study was conducted with primary-aged children in a very artificial laboratory situation. The punishments were loud noises of varying intensity. Whether these results are generalisable to disruptive adolescents is an empirical question which necessitates further study. However, Parke and other authors (Presland, 1980; Heron, 1978; Macmillan *et al.*, 1973), having reviewed the extant literature on the effectiveness of various forms of punishment, suggest that *implications* for classroom practice may be drawn, even from research on infra-human subjects in some cases.

Parke (1969) notes that five studies have demonstrated that the more delayed punishment is after the offence, the less effective it becomes. Research with infra-human subjects generally demonstrates that the more intense the punishment, the greater the suppressive effects thereof. However, as Parke's own (1969) study shows, the situation with human subjects is considerably more complex, although the generalisation *per se* still holds some validity for human applications. Thirdly, Parke notes that several studies with children have shown that punishment from a nurturant agent with whom the child has a good relationship is considerably more effective than punishment from a non-nurturing agent. It is perhaps worth noting that much of the classical research work on punishment is based on the notion that punishment arouses anxiety which generalises to other situations when the punishing agent is not present, thus achieving widespread inhibition of undesired behaviour. However, experience suggests that while this may be true of the majority of children, for those identified as severely disruptive it does not appear to apply, almost by definition. And as Parke's valuable (1969) study shows, there are complex interactions between the general trends in the ways punishment affects its subjects.

Heron (1978) notes that the effectiveness of response-cost procedures with 'emotionally disturbed' boys was demonstrated in two studies, whereby each rule infringement resulted in the loss of a pre-set amount of break or free time. Similar results were achieved with other populations of schoolchildren in four further studies.

From his review of the literature, Heron generates a list of 'guidelines' for the use of punishment, viz.

1. Aversive punishment usually suppresses, but only temporarily.
2. This short-term effect can reinforce teachers into using more and more aversive punishment, with less and less effect.
3. Aversive punishment may have undesirable side-effects, e.g. escape behaviour, emotional reaction, suppression of *wanted* behaviours, developing tolerance of increasing intensity of punishment or tolerance of a particular type of punishment, etc. Just as inhibition of

undesired behaviour can generalise to other children as a result of observing punishment of such behaviour in others, so can these damaging side-effects generalise.

4. Early punishment is more effective than delayed punishment. Just as positive reinforcement is more effective when the teacher has 'caught them being good', so punishment is more effective when administered directly upon their being 'bad'.

5. Remember that punishment merely suppresses undesired behaviour; it does not teach new behaviour.

6. Teachers utilising aversive punishment should remember that they are serving as models for the rest of their pupils, who may adopt similar techniques for use on fellow-pupils or teachers.

Macmillan *et al.* (1973), in a pro-punishment review of the research literature available at that time, reiterate the point that there are no universally effective punishments. However, they suggest that teachers require techniques other than extinction (ensuring non-reinforcement) of disruptive behaviour to couple with the accepted technique of re-inforcing desired behaviour. The point is made that, with disruptive children, the conditions for effective extinction of undesired behaviour can be difficult to arrange. However, Macmillan *et al.* certainly do not assume that punishment alone is effective. They do appear to assume that the conditions for *effective* punishment are easier to arrange in schools than the conditions for extinction, and this is perhaps debatable.

Concerning intensity of punishment, Macmillan *et al.* (1973) note that intense aversive punishment is only more effective than less intense punishment where the situation provides clearly discriminable alternatives for the children. Where children are confused about what they have done wrong and what they should be doing instead, more intense punishment may serve only to confuse and disturb them further. Macmillan *et al.* also note that there is some evidence that an initial fairly intense punishment is more effective than starting with a very mild aversive and gradually increasing the intensity of punishment. However, the evidence on this point is far from conclusive.

Macmillan *et al.* (1973) also address themselves to the question of consistency of punishment, a particular problem in secondary schools, where children are exposed to a large number of different teachers with different expectations and different management styles. It is noted that disruptive pupils have often received poor social training and been subject to erratic and inconsistent management at home, making the need for consistent management in the educational situation a prerequisite for even the slowest social relearning. In some cases disruptive behaviour at school may be positively approved of out of school and there is considerable evidence that the association of both reward and punishment with the same behaviour renders the behaviour much more resistant to extinction. Learning theory, of course, heavily emphasises the systematic and consistent implementation of programmed action.

Macmillan *et al.* (1973) concur with Heron (1978) on children's satiation with, and tolerance of, much-used punishments, and on the question of variation of punishment effectiveness according to the child's relationship with the punishing agent. In conclusion, they support the use of certain types of punishment as a means of increasing the effectiveness of a positively oriented programme of social training, when used in conjunction with such. As they point out, in the normal wear and tear of classroom management, teachers must ensure that the positive outweighs the negative, and particularly guard against 'holding grudges' which prevent them from positively reinforcing 'good' behaviour as soon as it occurs after a misdemeanour.

Presland (1980), although not taking an exhortatory pre-punishment stance, concurs with the conclusion of Macmillan *et al.*, and his paper particularly deals with English secondary schools. Presland, too, emphasises that the use of punishment should be planned and systematic, rather than an *ad hoc*, routine or despairing response to disruptive behaviour. Consistency and predictability are emphasised, as is clarity about the specific undesired behaviour *and* desired alternative behaviour.

Presland suggests a system of allocating various points to a range of offences, punishment being delivered when points have accumulated to a pre-specified level. (This system operates with footballing and driving offences, of course.) In addition, presumably a variety of punishments could be 'offered', each absorbing a different number of accumulated points. The specification of the latter would of course need to vary from pupil to pupil. However, the establishment of a systematic punishment system of this kind in a school would still prove largely ineffective if positive reinforcement for good behaviour were not also available, and to a greater degree than punishment. Presland's (1980) paper is particularly recommended to teachers for its brevity, simplicity and clarity.

Some teachers might argue that a positive rewards system would be unwieldy, time-consuming, inappropriate and ineffective. However, there is massive research evidence as to the effectiveness of positive reinforcement, and Milburn (1980) describes the use of such a scheme in a 2,000-strong split-site comprehensive school. Practical details of the operation of a merit and demerit scheme are provided, and Milburn notes that the scheme can be easily adapted to suit the needs of any school. Also relevant here is a reminder of the work of Ayllon and Roberts (1974), whose demonstration that disruptive behaviour can be reduced by reinforcing incompatible behaviour, i.e. academic perform-ance, should serve to encourage us not to dwell excessively or solely on 'the problem of disruptive behaviour', but to see it in the context of the functioning of the school as a whole.

Summary

Rewards systems are much more effective in producing good behaviour than punishment, which often makes little difference. Nevertheless, punishment is usually much more frequently employed in schools than rewards. What teachers intend to be punishing may not be so perceived by pupils, and increased disruption can result therefrom.

Verbal reprimands are useless if too frequent and can actually rein-force disruption. They can work if brief, specific, directive, stern and coupled with group praise for good behaviour. Quiet reprimands may be more effective than loud ones. Non-verbal displays of disapproval can be as effective as verbal reprimands.

Detention and 'lines' as usually operated make no difference to pupils' behaviour, and this is confirmed by the pupils themselves, except in Scotland. Carefully structured and systematic behavioural studies involving the loss of free time have shown much better effectiveness. These 'response-cost' procedures can apply to deprivation of other privi-leges, but the pupils have to have some privileges to be deprived of.

Despite the existence of massive research evidence that corporal punishment is at best ineffective and at worst damaging, there is no evidence that its use is declining other than very slowly. Such punish-ment is often used inconsistently, and there is evidence that the use of unofficial physical punishment is particularly likely to result in worse behaviour. To some extent its use may serve to deter other children from offending, but there are ethical objections here, and the children themselves do not consider it particularly effective. Disruptive children are in any case likely to be the most resistant to such punishment. There is no evidence that behaviour deteriorates in schools where corporal punishment is abandoned.

On the whole, the children regard punishments involving contact with their parents as the most effective. Older pupils are generally more sceptical about the effectiveness of all punishments.

In general, punishment may sometimes suppress behaviour, but only briefly, and this can result in over-use of punishment by teachers. No one punishment is effective for all pupils. Punishment shows more effectiveness where: (1) it is immediate (especially with mild sanctions); (2) the recipient regards the punisher as 'caring', and has a good relationship with him/her (especially with immediate sanctions); (3) it is consistent, systematic and predictable; (4) the undesired behaviour is not positively reinforced elsewhere; (5) there is clear specification of undesired and desired alternative behaviour, and attempts are made to train towards the latter as well as punish the former; (6) the punishment is intense and has commenced at a fairly high level of intensity, but only where (5) also applies; and the interaction can be complex. The damaging effects of punishment can include escape behaviour, adverse emotional reaction, suppression of desired behaviours, development of tolerance of punishments of increasing intensity, satiation with oft-repeated punishments, and copying of punishing behaviour by pupils.

There is massive research evidence that reward systems result in better outcomes than punishment, and schoolchildren agree with this finding although teachers usually do not. Children regard rewards involving parents as the most effective, and also favour time off lessons and extra preferred lessons. Rewards are likely to be effective where pupils see they are earned by good behaviour, rather than distributed randomly.

Early reward is more effective than delayed reward. Verbal praise from teachers can be an effective reward, but public praise tends to be reacted to adversely by some older pupils, especially boys. Non-verbal approval can be as effective as verbal praise.

Children quite favour prizes as rewards, but the evidence suggests this to be more effective with academic achievement than behaviour. However, reinforcing academic performance can result in a decrease in incompatible disruptive behaviour in some pupils.

Clear and specific behavioural requirements, consistently and systematically applied, are associated with better behaviour.

21 MISCELLANEOUS

The range of suggestions for action to combat disruption is extremely wide. A mid-week disco and a tuck-shop have been suggested, to combat disruption arising from irritability owing to lack of breakfast and disruption' arising from mid-week boredom (equidistance from weekends) (*Times Educational Supplement*, 1981). The same report suggests staggering morning break to reduce the numbers in the corridors, setting up display units to encourage respect for each other's work, and extending link courses and work experience programmes.

Leeds City Council (1975) suggests dispersing disruptive children to separate classes, transferring them to other ordinary schools, operating a variety of 'reporting' systems, mounting 'motivation courses' (for pupils), and sundry 'therapeutic activities'. The DES (1978a) note that one school claimed that team teaching reduced disruption.

Garibaldi (1979) documents various other approaches in the USA. One is to have an Ombudsperson who is appointed to mediate in disputes between students and teachers, teachers and parents, parents and administrators, and so on. Some schools operate 'after-school counselling clinics' which students can attend to help resolve their problems without using up valuable class-time. Some schools have 'pupil problem teams', comprising counsellor, social worker, psychologist and often a parent, who visit schools on a regular or *ad hoc* basis. Other schools have 'work-study programmes', whereby pupils may 'work-off' a suspension by doing chores after school – detention with hard labour. This system has been extended to having Saturday school and evening school in California – superdetention.

NASSP (1976) reports on similar detention systems, known as 'behaviour clinics'. Also described is an anti-vandalism scheme whereby a fixed fund is set aside per school for the repair of vandalism, and what is left at the end of the school year can be spent by the student body on equipment to be used in school for their pleasure. A student-teacher committee inspects damage to determine if it was the result of vandalism. Another school has a 'youth service bureau' manned by two policemen, who also teach some classes and take some extra-curricular activities. It seems that a number of high schools have resident police officers in some guise or other, and some schools even employ private security personnel to control vandalism and disruption. Some other high schools have preferred to accentuate the positive by issuing co-operative students with 'Honor Passes' or by offering membership of the 'Citizenship Honor Society', which results in certain privileges becoming available. Passes or membership are suspended or cancelled if a student gets into trouble.

Illera (1977) describes a programme for 'disturbed adolescents in a day facility' wherein children had 'simulated work experience' — they were paid to do work on a contract basis for the school, and level of pay was based on quality of work and acceptability of behaviour while on-task. The other feature of this programme was 'group evaluation meetings', where all the participants gathered to see if they could be co-operative and behave well in this situation, and to increase their awareness of their behaviour. The group members would set behavioural targets for each other, and later evaluate whether or not targets had been met.

Smith (1973) describes various other strategies in use in the USA. These include having a shorter school day, having pupils lunch out of school, and having a system of certain members of staff 'befriending' disruptive pupils. However, none of the miscellaneous suggestions and programmes referred to so far offer any evaluative data as to effectiveness. Shores and Hambrich (1969) at least attempted this in their study of the effectiveness of having disruptive pupils work in cubicles. They found that a significant increase in attending behaviour resulted, although academic achievement showed no improvement.

Rutter *et al.* (1979) found that pupils' behaviour was better where teachers started lessons promptly, did not take time to hand out materials, stuck to the lesson topic, taught the group rather than individuals, sometimes made the class work silently, and did not finish lessons early.

However, there is some evidence on various miscellaneous factors which *do not* make any difference to the functioning of school pupils. In a review of studies of class size and achievement in school, Hedderly (1981) notes that there is no evidence that smaller class sizes make any difference to learning progress. These findings are confirmed by Rutter *et al.* (1979), who found that pupils' attendance, behaviour and attainment *did not* vary with size of staff-pupil ratio or size of teaching groups, nor with whether the pastoral care system was house-based or year-based, nor with whether mixed-ability or setted teaching was operating, nor with size of school, nor with whether the school had split sites.

Summary

Having disruptive pupils work in cubicles increases their attention to the task.

There is no evidence that small class size reduces disruptive behaviour. The same applies to small school size.

RESOURCE CONTINUA

The concept of a continuum of provision was discussed in the Introduction, and subsequent chapters dealing with individual types of provision were arranged in order of decreasing cost and restrictiveness to the pupil. In this chapter, authorities and school boards who have set up resources which offer a variety of types of provision in a co-ordinated and flexible way will be considered.

In 1966, Morse described his model for a 'school-based psychoeducational team', which would operate from a centre containing a 'diagnostic class', a long-term class, in-service training accommodation, specialised materials resource bank, library and special aids loan service. The centre would be staffed by special teachers, psychologists and social workers. The main function of the team would be to 'help the school accommodate a wider variety of children', and to that end the staff would spend more time in ordinary schools or working with parents than they would in the centre.

Klein *et al.* (1967) describe such a programme in Tucson, Arizona, in which resources included a residential school with two classes, a day school with six classes for 60 children, four special classes in elementary schools, support teachers who offered daily counselling and 'therapy' to 60 children, a recreational therapy programme and an in-service training programme for teachers in ordinary schools, attendance at which was a compulsory contractual obligation. However, no evaluation of any kind of this large operation is reported.

The 3R programme is described by Pearl (1979) and Skinski *et al.* (1978). Pearl notes how six levels of resource of increasing expense and restrictiveness are available. Skinski *et al.* describe how this provision for behaviour-difficulty children follows the resource-continuum model already operating in many parts of the USA for learning-difficulty children. Liaison Teacher-Counsellors (LTCs) support and maintain disruptive children in the ordinary school environment. Counselling, contracting and behaviour modification techniques are used within the total ecology of the problem child, and much energy is devoted to in-service training with teachers and parents. The LTCs aim to modify and co-ordinate the efforts of the people making up the disruptive student's day-to-day environment. They observe base-rates of behaviour, advise about behavioural programmes and techniques, provide suggestions about learning materials, monitor the child's daily progress, and so on. If this level of intervention fails, children may be withdrawn from some lessons for one-to-one teaching, counselling or remedial help by the LTC. If this fails, the LTC may arrange resource-room placement to occupy a larger part of the child's timetable. If this fails, short-term (6-8 months) out-of-school units are available, and if these fail, longer-term units (1-3 years) are available. While children are in these units, work with the child's natural ecology is continued, indeed is claimed to increase, since an early return to the least restrictive environment is the goal of all efforts. Reintroduction to ordinary classes is gradual, and initially on a part-time basis.

Skinski *et al.* (1978) claim that increased academic attainment and behavioural gains have been achieved by this programme. Of the most difficult pupils, for whom some unit provision was made, academic gains of twice the average in both reading and maths are recorded, and these results have been maintained over several years. On behavioural checklists, students entered the units with an average of 11 out of 14 factors checked. On follow-up back in the ordinary schools, this had been reduced to an average of 2 out of 14 factors. Unfortunately no evaluation results for those children seen only by LTCs in the ordinary school are presented.

The Alachua County Schools (1975) programme has already been referred to at various points in this book. Five different 'instructional models' (i.e. educational systems) for disruptive pupils were tried out over a two-year period, and comparatively evaluated. (Would that all education authorities proceeded in the same orderly manner.)

Five objectives were stipulated for attainment by all five models. The first was to increase the rate of appropriate behaviour on a rating scale completed by the ordinary classteachers, increase the pupils' social skills as measured in a precision teaching model, observational data and a self-concept scale, and improve academic skills as measured by two achievement tests and data from precision teaching records. The second was to return students to ordinary classes full time with the skills for successful continuance of the placement. The third was to provide in-service training for all teachers involved with disruptive children on the management of such children, and the fourth was to provide more formal in-service training on curriculum development for such children. The fifth objective was to provide training and support to the parents of disruptive children.

The alternative systems of service delivery were: off-site units, in-school resource rooms, 'crisis intervention rooms', itinerant support

teachers, and 'diagnostic-prescriptologists' (consultants). It is unfortunately unclear how children were allocated to the different types of
provision, and this study is of cross-sample comparisons rather than an
evaluation of a continuum of resources.

The off-site units contained both acting-out and withdrawn children
in the average ratio of 3:2. The practical advantages were that a high
degree of structure and individualisation of management were possible.
The disadvantages were that the setting was unnatural, it was difficult
to get the children back into ordinary school, there were transport problems, the units tended to be used as dumping grounds, the 'labelling'
resulted in permanent endorsement of children's records, and there
were no 'normal' peer models. The units were only intended for a very
few highly disruptive children, but the setting was still too restrictive for
some children placed there. Liaison and consultation with the ordinary
schools were difficult, the children modelled on each other's inappropriate behaviour, and despite the high degree of structure, problems of
control were still encountered. More specifically evaluative data showed
that 'at least half' of the students showed normal behaviour *in the
special unit* within one year. Academically, two-thirds made attainment
gains which were at least 'normal', i.e. equal to gain in chronological
age. However, the rate of return from the off-site units to ordinary
school was very low indeed. Later evaluative data showed that the proportion of children whose behaviour could be stabilised *within* the unit
rose to 75 per cent, but academic gains showed a marked decline, with
no pupils making 'normal' gains. It is not clear whether this change was
due to alteration in the staffing or intake of the units.

The resource rooms operated on the understanding that the room
was a resource to students and teachers alike. All students were part
time. The practical advantages were that the resource was immediately
available, there were no transition problems, support for the ordinary
teacher was readily available, and a greater number of children could
be served. The main disadvantage lay in the difficulty of co-ordinating
timetabling, and some dumping could still occur. This model was used
for the majority of disruptive children. Specific evaluative data showed
that less than half the pupils had achieved normal behaviour by the
end of the year — but of course this was within the ordinary school.
Academically, two-thirds showed normal or higher gains. Children spent
a maximum of only 12 hours per week in the resource room. Thus, a
higher case load was served, and the rate of full-time return to ordinary
classes was much higher than from the off-site units.

The 'crisis intervention rooms' suffered from great unclarity as to what the crisis teacher was supposed to *do*, and had the danger of reinforcing crisis situations. Very close relationships with ordinary teachers were necessary for this model to be at all effective, and these were not always enjoyed. There were problems of role unclarity, and complaints about duplication of services. Only a highly competent person could operate in this way successfully. Problems of organisation eventually resulted in children being timetabled to see the 'crisis teacher'! The crisis teacher spent much time 'consulting' with ordinary class teachers, but it is not clear on what theoretical or empirical basis. Evaluation results suggested that ordinary teachers saw random fluctuations in behaviour, although a majority of children were said to show some improvement (? spontaneous remission). Academically, only a third of the children made normal achievement gains.

The itinerant support programme was intended to support classteachers, mobilise community resources, work with parents and help to promote academic skills. This model had the advantage of serving even more students (i.e. was even cheaper), was an in-service resource and helped ordinary classteachers solve problems. The difficulties were that good relations were not establishable everywhere and there was alienation from some ordinary schools, and that the service seemed spread too thin. Effectiveness was found to depend on the case load of the itinerant teacher. In this programme, each itinerant teacher had two schools, and spent two days in one and three days in another. Although many UK services operating on this model would regard this level of provision as luxurious, the Alachua Schools considered that this resulted in insufficient time and insufficient reinforcement for the pupils and ordinary school teachers. Less than half the pupils in this programme moved towards or attained normal behaviour, and only one-third made normal or better academic gains. However, these results are very similar to those achieved by the 'crisis teachers', at about half the cost. It is, however, worse than spontaneous remission rate. It is not known what theoretical or empirical model was used by the itinerant teachers.

The 'diagnostic-prescriptologists' served an even larger number of schools, and spent on average one day per week in each school. They had a purely advisory, consultative role, and made suggestions, mapped out programmes and recording systems, and generally offered support, advice and training to ordinary classteachers. There were obviously no transition and reintegration problems with this model, but some teachers felt threatened by it, and it seemed effective only for mildly disruptive pupils. For some reason, results of pre- and post-testing are not available for this model.

The parental support aspect of these programmes proved to be something of a failure. Parent training and support groups met, individual conferences were held with parents, home visits for counselling were made, etc., but the level of parental response and contact was generally poor. One point that did emerge was that contact with parents needed to concentrate on structured topics and objectives − merely talking 'shop' or talking round problems was largely useless.

As a result of this evaluation, Alachua Schools decided to maintain only the two forms of intervention which had been found to be most effective, namely off-site units and in-school resource rooms, in their case. These were, of course, the most expensive resources, and the Alachua Schools' decision to focus on two elements of their range of resource types appears to negate the possibility of ensuring that expensive resources are only used where absolutely necessary, i.e. where a cheaper resource is proven to be ineffective. Of the two resources which were retained, the in-school resource rooms were far more effective in achieving the programme's second objective, satisfactory full-time return to ordinary classes, and appeared to be substantially more *cost*-effective than off-site units overall.

Turning to developments in the UK, we find that programmes are on a much smaller scale and show greater flexibility. Lane and Millar (1977) describe the work of the Hungerford (now 'Islington') Educational Guidance Centre. The theoretical basis is 'on behavioural lines within the framework of contract therapy'. Very close work with the ordinary school is the essence of the mode of operation. Initially problem clarification and data-gathering are undertaken with all parties, and objectives for change set and agreed. All parties involved then work towards the agreed changes. In the course of this, centre staff may teach the child at the centre for part of the week, or in the ordinary school for part of the week, but in some cases might not be greatly involved with the child at all. Lane and Millar cite various case studies, but no overall evaluative data are given, although every case involvement is evaluated in terms of the objectives initially agreed for it.

A wide range of evaluative data is presented by David Lane in a later publication (Lane, 1983), which addresses itself to a number of issues emerging from his work. Lane's long-term data demonstrate that children presenting conduct disorders in school show a high subsequent rate of delinquency at five-year follow-up. He implies that effective intervention in this chain of events, assuming that there *is* some direct causal link, can thus be of substantial subsequent benefit to society, irrespective of any short-term benefit to pupil or host school. Evidence to support this is cited from a comparison of 40 'centre' pupils with 40 controls in terms of convictions over a 10-year period, the 'centre' pupils doing substantially better in the long run.

A five-year follow-up study of 69 pupils seen by teachers as having either anxiety or conduct problems confirms findings from elsewhere that spontaneous remission rates for children with acting-out behavioural problems may be expected to be worse than those for children with neurotic, under-reactive problems. In an investigation of the efficacy of a range of traditional interventions and 'treatments', Lane (1983) reports a three-year follow-up of 114 pupils recorded as experiencing a range of problems, some of whom received no outside help, while the other group encountered child guidance treatment, tutorial classes, off-site units, etc. (but *not* Lane's own centre). While the 'treated' group did show slightly better outcomes at follow-up, these differences did not reach statistical significance.

Set against this general trend, Lane's (1983) data show encouraging improvement in children who had experienced intervention by the centre. Total over-reaction scores on Bristol Social Adjustment Guides for 40 'centre' pupils, before intervention and six months after intervention, were compared to those of children experiencing 'other treatments'. Initial and final scores for centre children, all of whom had had some direct teaching from centre staff in or out of the centre, differed significantly in a positive direction, but no significant improvements emerged for the other group. There is evidence that on the whole these gains are sustained at three-year follow-up. Although of course not *all* 'centre' pupils improved, those that did improve appeared to maintain their gains, while those that did not failed to show even a 'spontaneous remission' improvement after three years had elapsed. Data are also available on re-referral and suspension rates for 50 'centre' pupils and 50 receiving 'other treatments', with both rates proving substantially and significantly lower for 'centre' pupils.

A not dissimilar operation is described by Berryman *et al.* (1980). Past experience had shown that in-school special classes resulted in the special teachers becoming too isolated, while long-term withdrawal to off-site units resulted in 'curriculum deprivation' and reintegration problems. Nevertheless, it was felt that a totally itinerant support service might lead to fragmentation of the service, so a combination of off-site withdrawal and in-school itinerant support is now being offered. Part-time withdrawal to the centre and centre staff teaching disruptive children in the ordinary school are permutations which do not occur frequently in this case, however, although there is considerable emphasis

on flexibility. Children who do attend the centre do so for a short nego-
tiated period which may be as short as two or three weeks, and is only
three months on average. Centre staff are heavily involved in developing
management programmes for disruptive children in ordinary schools at
both secondary and primary level, although mostly the latter, and these
are usually of a behaviour modification type. Training in interpersonal
social and coping skills is offered directly to some pupils in the centre.
In one or two cases, the objective is set to increase academic attainment, but usually this is not expected to result from a brief stay in the
centre, with its inevitably restricted curriculum. Although each case
can be evaluated within itself, no overall evaluative data are available.
However, almost all children return to ordinary schools, with a very few
continuing into special schools.

Coulby (1980) describes the work of a 'Schools Support Unit', staffed
by 12 teachers, teacher-in-charge, educational psychologist and senior
education welfare officer. The unit staff might intervene with ordinary
school management (senior) staff, with ordinary school classteachers,
with the child, with the parents, or with any combination of these, each
in a variety of ways. However, the unit attempts to work to a hierarchy
of interventions, and every attempt is made to implement the intervention that causes least upset to the life of the child and least expenditure
of resources, compatible with effectiveness.

Methods employed include assessment and clarification of problems
with teachers, and co-ordinating their management of a pupil. Closer
involvement can include implementation and/or monitoring of a behavioural programme by the unit teacher, in the context of a team-
teaching situation if necessary. The unit teacher may become involved
in individual or group counselling with disruptive children, social skills
training or reciprocal behaviour contracting. Liaison, counselling or contracting with parents may also be undertaken. If necessary, pupils may
be withdrawn part time to the special class at the support unit. This
class is staffed by one teacher for five mornings and by a second teacher
for three afternoons per week. Pupils normally attend for three or five
sessions per week, over a period which is very rarely any longer than
eight weeks, and often much shorter. Other teachers in the team also
teach in the class part time, which allows them to keep in touch with
pupils for whose cases they are responsible, broadens the curriculum and
adds interpersonal variety, and provides support for the regular special
class teachers. Attempts are made to keep pupils' work programmes related to those in the feeder secondary schools.

Evaluation procedures have been built into the operation of the unit for some time. Behaviour checklists of various sorts are completed by the ordinary school teachers during the assessment phase directly after referral, and again after the intervention when the unit's involvement in a case is being terminated. While longer-term follow-up is not specifically mentioned, schools are able to re-refer pupils whose behaviour gains are not maintained back to the unit, which was not the case in the centre described by Berryman *et al.* (1980). Coulby (1980) accepts that these evaluation results may well be clouded by the operation of other variables in addition to the intervention of the unit, but nevertheless this work appears to represent the most substantial evaluation so far of a programme of this kind in the UK.

Coulby and Harper's (1981) Phase I evaluation report is a clear, detailed and wide-ranging document. It should be noted by way of background that while their support unit operated in a socially deprived area, the division *also* had two day schools for 'maladjusted' children, five 'tutorial classes', five 'intermediate education centres' for children with school attendance problems, an 'education guidance centre', facilities for home tuition, and five special classes within individual secondary schools, all catering in some way for some pupils who might be deemed 'disruptive'. The relationship of the support unit to the rest of this provision must thus have been complex, and possibly unclear. The objectives of the whole ILEA scheme of funding of various provisions are cited as: (1) to find educationally acceptable ways of dealing with pupils who disrupt their education and that of others; (2) to reduce the need for corporal and other severe punishments; (3) to reduce the number of pupils suspended. The aims of the support unit are somewhat differently slanted, however: 'the first and over-riding responsibility of the team is to facilitate the best education appropriate to the needs of the child, whilst at the same time attempting to minimise his/her interference with the schooling of other children, and the amount of undue stress under which teachers are placed'.

In the first two years of operation of the support unit (February 1979 to February 1981), 333 children were referred from 14 secondary and 54 primary schools. There were about equal numbers of primary and secondary-aged children referred. However, more primary-aged cases (110) had been closed at the end of Phase I than secondary-aged (72), indicating that the unit had less success with the adolescent population which is our immediate focus of interest. The study contains evidence that behavioural change was particularly difficult to achieve with 14- to 15-year-olds, but to a lesser extent the 8- to 9-year-old group also proved less tractable on intervention than children of other ages. More children tended to be referred at these apparently 'difficult' ages than at others. A total of 75 per cent of referrals were of boys, but outcomes for boys and girls were not found to differ significantly. Most children did seem to be referred for 'acting-out', assertive behaviour problems, rather than being neurotic, withdrawn and 'under-reactive'. There were differences in the type of intervention most commonly employed at primary and secondary levels: secondary intervention tended to be more oriented towards withdrawing pupils from classes in schools, withdrawing them into the unit class, and counselling them (often behaviourally) in school, while at the primary level there was more emphasis on observation in class, advice to teachers and behavioural programming.

The mean length of support unit involvement in a case was 22 to 23 weeks. Taking the crude measure of re-referral rates as an index of successful intervention, of 161 children still in school and in the area at case closure, 129 (80 per cent) were not re-referred to the support unit or the Psychological Service owing to initial problem recurrence. On Bristol Social Adjustment Guides (n = 30), acting-out behaviour significantly dropped from referral to case closure. On a purpose-developed behavioural checklist (n = 24), a mean reduction from 39 to 26 points from referral to closure was found, again statistically significant. Follow-up data were available 6 months after closure on only a very few cases, but the trends were most encouraging, indicating continuing decline in problem behaviour.

In addition to these measures, teachers were asked to complete post-intervention questionnaires when cases were closed, and further evaluative data were thus garnered from teacher perceptions. Questionnaires were available for 90 cases. Each one asked the teacher to rate improvement or deterioration in five behaviours targeted for change which were specific to that child's case. Some 77.7 per cent of the children were reported to have improved, 20 per cent stayed the same and 2.3 per cent deteriorated. Although teacher perceptions may not represent the 'hardest' of evaluative data, as referrals are initiated on the basis of teacher perceptions it is not unreasonable to evaluate case intervention by a more structured usage of the same data-base. The 78 per cent 'improvement rate' compares very favourably with spontaneous remission, but Coulby and Harper (1981) unfortunately do not give separate data for the secondary age group.

The post-intervention questionnaires also indicated that 38 per cent of the teachers thought *the rest of the class* had improved behaviourally, and 39 per cent thought the rest of the class had improved academically, as a result of the intervention. These figures seem curiously low in relation to the improvement rates for the behaviour of the referred child, and perhaps suggest that individual children may too readily be seen as the 'cause' of poor behaviour and academic progress in the rest of the class. There are no data on the post-intervention academic progress of the referred children, an area to which other studies of different systems have paid considerable attention. Some 57 per cent of the teachers reported that they felt more confident as a result of the intervention, although few reported feeling under any less pressure as a result of it. Curiously, while there was no evidence that particular members of the support team tended to produce more successful behavioural outcomes than others, there was some difference between the support teachers in ability to inspire feelings of confidence in the ordinary schoolteachers. Successful outcome seemed to bear no relationship to length of involvement, but in a situation where the model of working implies that the support teacher keeps working through a hierarchy of interventions until success is achieved, this would not be particularly expected.

In Phase I, data were too sparse to permit a valid assessment of relative effectiveness of different types of intervention. However, in Phase II, Coulby and Harper (1983) report fuller data on another 100 cases, which offer some indices of differential outcome according to the nature of support team input. A general trend seems to be that there is an inverse relationship between improvement rates and age for each type of intervention, so that the older the child at point of referral, the more heavily resourced the input needs to be to effect behavioural change.

The Phase II data in general broadly confirm the encouraging results of Phase I, and further details of the former are worth close scrutiny. It seems clear that a unit operating on flexible resource-continuum lines can provide a cost-effective service.

Summary

There is evidence from the UK and USA that a resource continuum, offering services ranging from total withdrawal of the child from classes through to advisory support and training work with classteachers, can prove very effective. Such an operation need not be large, providing it is flexible, and certainly fits well with the concept of placement in the least restrictive environment, and with ensuring economic use of resources and maximum cost-effectiveness. Some research implies that it is necessary for a service for disruptive children to be able to offer some direct teaching for the most disruptive children, although whether the capability of providing full-time off-site provision is necessary is debatable. The existence of resource continua helps facilitate the transfer of off-site gains to the ordinary school environment. In the UK, the Islington EGC and Tower Hamlets Support Unit model looks very promising, and local authorities will doubtless be very interested in the full data (Lane, 1983; Coulby and Harper, 1983). Within the UK, service 'continua' are reported to operate on largely behavioural problem-solving lines.

Part Seven

CONCLUSIONS

23 SUMMARY

Residential special schools in the UK show average learning gains and poor behavioural gains within the school, and have poor reintegration rates. Better results are reported from the USA.

Day special schools show worse learning gains and worse behaviour gains within the school, and have similarly poor reintegration rates. In the very few cases where a high proportion *are* reintegrated, subsequent adjustment is good. Subsequent employment prospects are quite good.

Separate units show very varied learning gains, but curricula are restricted and overall results poor. Reintegration rates are very poor on the whole, and subsequent adjustment is well below spontaneous remission rates.

Separate units with transition facilities and part-time attendance have shown equivalent academic gains and better reintegration rates and subsequent adjustment, but only in the USA.

'Alternative schools' do not lend themselves to evaluation, and there is little evidence that they are effective.

Suspension of pupils has not been shown to be an effective practice, and off-site suspension units merely greatly increase the time suspended pupils spend out of mainstream education. In-school fixed-period suspension units do better, but still no better than spontaneous remission.

Special classes have shown good learning gains on full-time or part-time bases in the USA, but these gains tend to disappear at follow-up. Only behaviourally organised classes have shown continuity and generalisation of gains. In the UK, special classes appear to have done little to ease stress in schools, and have had reintegration problems.

Resource rooms have shown good learning and behavioural gains, but these have also tended to have disappeared within two years. However, the resource room has fewer reintegration problems.

Time-out rooms have shown a high degree of effectiveness, providing their usage is methodical and consistent.

'Crisis rooms' or 'crisis teachers' have not attracted, or proved amenable to, evaluation, and there is no evidence that they can be effective.

In-school support teachers may be effective if they operate on a clearly structured, behaviourally oriented model.

Paraprofessionals and adult community volunteers *can* be quite as effective as professionals in helping disruptive children. However, evaluation results are very mixed, and there is limited evidence on effectiveness with disruptive secondary-school pupils.

Volunteer peers using behavioural techniques have shown substantial effectiveness in a variety of ways, although relatively few studies give evidence of long-term gains.

Itinerant support teachers have been the subject of limited research, but clearly do not have a reintegration problem. They appear cost-effective, particularly where operating on behavioural lines, and can have a positive effect on the whole organisation of the ordinary school.

Consultants may reassure teachers, but have shown limited effectiveness in changing teacher behaviour and thereby the disruptive behaviour of the pupils. Effective consultation is intensive, structured, group-based and behaviourally oriented, and may not be distinguishable from in-service training.

In-service training for teachers in the management of disruptive children is most effective within a behavioural framework, although courses dealing with intra-school organisation and communication can also be useful.

Pupil training in pro-social behaviour by behavioural means has produced good results, but in only half of the cases have these gains endured in the long term. Self-recording systems have proved effective in helping pupils control their behaviour, and self-reinforcement has been shown to be as effective as teacher reinforcement.

Parent training can prove more effective in changing disruptive pupils' behaviour than working directly with the children, particularly so via the utilisation of behavioural methodology. Home-school liaison has been shown to be highly cost-effective.

Curriculum has an influence on disruptive behaviour. Flexible, individualised curricula, with structured objectives and built-in reinforcement, can reduce disruption.

Routine sanctions of a traditional kind are by definition ineffective with most disruptive pupils. Punishment is not usually effective, and reward systems are much more effective in changing behaviour. What teachers intend as punishment may be reinforcing. Sanctions involving contact with parents are the most effective, much more so than corporal punishment. There is substantial discussion of the effectiveness of various rewards and punishments in Chapter 20.

Resource continua, offering a flexible range of services from total withdrawal of the child through to advisory support and training work with ordinary teachers, can prove very effective, and they are certainly organisationally well placed to ensure generalisation and duration of gains, and maximise cost-effectiveness. Again, the behaviourally oriented operations demonstrate highest effectiveness.

24 DISCUSSION

At this juncture the patient reader who has painstakingly plodded the tortuous path through all these dusty research findings must be applauded — rare indeed in the field of education is such perseverance and professional commitment! The need for an aura of objectivity has disallowed the author from any diversionary forays into whimsy or satire, which might have offered a degree of light relief. Of course, attempts were made to help the reader digest the whale — the skeletal structure of the Contents Cascade, the Introduction, the Chapter summaries and overall Summary should all have helped with orientation. Let us now confront the beast in its entirety.

Inevitably, confusions have arisen along the way. Much of the categorisation of projects into chapters has inescapably been somewhat arbitrary. This has been particularly true where the attempt to focus on 'systems' of service delivery has been debilitated by the difficulties inherent in discussing projects which are essentially evaluations of particular methods or techniques operating within a *given* system context. Notwithstanding this confusion, it has emerged clearly that behavioural methods or techniques consistently do particularly well in terms of effectiveness, and that this applies virtually irrespective of system context. That this is so may reflect little more than the fact that the conceptual framework of behaviourism lends itself especially well to the evaluative process. Behavioural psychology asks questions that can be answered! While none but the most ardent behaviourist would assert that behavioural psychology can ever offer a total explanation of the deeper complexities of human experience, there can be no doubt that for many everyday practical purposes, it works. It can be argued that those who seek a more grandiose and emotionally satisfying psychology, which affords *Homo sapiens* vastly more dignity than his fellow mammals, should conduct their search at their own expense.

The use of a spontaneous remission rate of approximately two-thirds as an evaluative touchstone will also doubtless have raised a hackle or two. Surely, it can be argued, studies finding such a rate of spontaneous remission have tended to look at large numbers of children with very various behavioural difficulties. Are the results of such studies really relevant to the kind of children served by many of the facilities here under discussion — the hardest of the hard-core disruptives? The fallacy

160

here is the old assumption that the word 'disruptive' has some fixed, agreed or homogeneous meaning. But, in fact, children are labelled 'disruptive' in some classes but not in others; in school but not at home (or vice versa); in some education authorities but not others; now but not 6 months ago and not in 12 months' time. The 'hardest of the hard core' may have arrived at the doubtful privilege of this social rank purely by chance. In the event, while it is true that some of the studies of the 'prognosis' for various forms of 'social pathology' in adolescents have cast their net rather wider than is immediately relevant to our current focus of concern, there are still several studies which have demonstrated the existence of the 66 per cent spontaneous remission rate in populations of severely disruptive and delinquent adolescents. The procedure of comparing success rates of various programmes to a nominal 66 per cent spontaneous remission rate, as adopted in this book, would thus seem justified for all studies where well-matched control groups were not used.

The corollary of acceptance of the existence of spontaneous remission is the realisation that some forms of intervention must therefore actually make things *worse* than they would otherwise be. Or to put it another way, as spontaneous remission has a 66 per cent chance of operating anyway, doing nothing may be the best form of action. Doing nothing may certainly be better than setting up a very expensive facility which has no positive effects and possibly some negative ones. It does not appear to be true that 'any action is better than none', although citation of this beguiling fallacy may well make uninformed decision-makers *feel* better. There may thus be something to be said for 'radical non-intervention'. Carrying the analogy further, for some facilities we might get beyond the zero point where facilities have no impact at all, into the realms of 'negative cost-effectiveness', or 'cost-damage', so comparisons could be made of the cheapest system for doing a given amount of harm to the education of disruptive children.

With these considerations in mind, a diagrammatic over-view of relative cost of the various 'systems' and facilities discussed may be helpful. This takes the form of an expanded Reinert-type 'cascade'.

Many teachers may be a little surprised to note from this mapping how few of the range of systems are dependent on off-site physical provision, and how many operable within the context of the ordinary school.

The 'total cascade' displays a hierarchy of interventions of increasing cost and restrictiveness. But as the evaluation research demonstrates, the more expensive interventions are not necessarily the more effective.

Figure 2. The Total Cascade

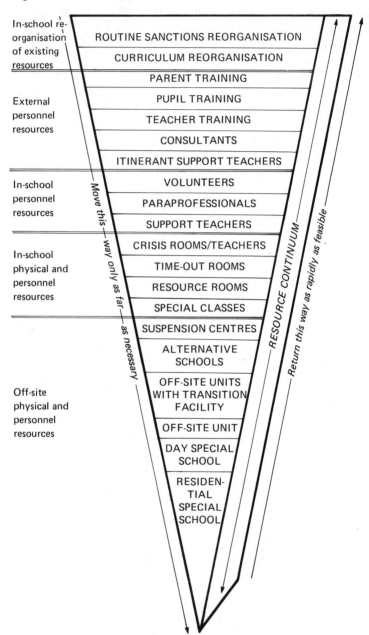

The various systems considered might be roughly grouped according to *cost*-effectiveness thus:

BEST BUYS
Time-out
Parent training (home-school liaison)
Resource continua

WORTH TRYING
Routine sanction change
Curriculum change
Pupil training — in self-recording
Peer volunteers
In-service training
Itinerant support teachers
Resource rooms
Separate part-time units with transition facilities

DOUBTFUL
Consultants
Adult volunteers
Paraprofessionals
Pupil training — group counselling
Pupil training — social skills
In-school special classes
In-school support teachers

STRICTLY LUXURY CLASS
Crisis rooms and teachers
Suspension units
Alternative schools
Separate units
Day special schools
Residential special schools

It is unrealistic to expect any educational organisation to be able to provide the full range of 'total cascade' services, nor does the evidence suggest that such an approach would prove managerially sound or economical. However, if the admittedly dubious banding of systems noted above can be accepted for the purposes of thought clarification, it becomes possible to produce a 'cost-effective cascade', thus:

Figure 3. Cost-effective Cascade

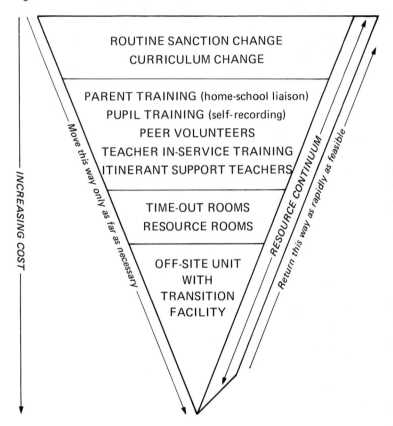

Some education authorities or organisations may not be able to generate sufficient resource allocation priority to establish anything which remotely resembles a cascade or continuum. This would be unfortunate, since the work of Lane (1983) and Coulby and Harper (1983) shows that a flexible resource continuum offering a reasonably wide range of services to a high degree of effectiveness can be established with limited resources. It may be that some authorities will have heavy capital (and, in some cases, emotional) investment tied up in long-established physical resources which cannot be dismantled without political embarrassment. This clearly constitutes a managerial problem concerning effective re-allocation of resources, rather than implying any need to conjure up 'extra' resources for a 'new' venture, which overlays the redundant paraphernalia of a previous era when administrative decisions were based even less on evaluative evidence than is currently the case.

For whatever reason, in some areas the 'system' provision available will be fragmentary and ill co-ordinated. There may be huge gaps in resourcing between service systems of wildly differing intensities. Some authorities, for example, may only offer consultants (perhaps in the form of educational or school psychologists) and places at residential special schools. Not only does this build in an inevitable degree of automatic failure (and therefore loss of credibility in other spheres of work) for the consultants, but it results in some children being placed in a very expensive resource unnecessarily, and possibly damagingly.

The implementation of a cost-effective cascade should maximise utility gained for a given outlay. It also gives the structure of a sequence or hierarchy of possible interventions, which in turn makes the implementation of sequential strategies in dealing with disruptive adolescents possible, instead of the *ad hoc* straw-clutching which can characterise operations in this area. Teachers have the security of knowing there is a co-ordinated system for dealing with disruptive pupils, which may improve their confidence to a degree which reduces the demand upon the system. Pupils also know there is an agreed and co-ordinated system, which may make them hesitate in their attempts to out-manipulate the organisation.

The availability of a sequence of strategies of proven effectiveness also implies that the labelling and categorisation of children for administrative purposes becomes totally functionless and irrelevant. Attempts to explain disruptive behaviour in terms of deficits within the child also become irrelevant. There is no need to try to predict how a child will behave in a different environment. The cascade enables testing of the hypothesis that a certain form of intervention will work. If that intervention proves insufficient for that particular pupil, at that particular time, the next intervention on the hierarchy can be tried on the same empirical basis. Thus the cascade or continuum is operated on the basis of formulating, testing and re-formulating hypotheses. This is also known as the 'suck-it-and-see' model.

The cascade also offers schools indications of actions which might be construed as 'preventive'. Thus, changes in the organisation of the curriculum or routine sanctions might create changes in the ethos and routine of the school, which not only reduce the incidence of disruptiveness in the school in general, including that contributed by pupils who are infrequent offenders, but which also improve the quality of education for all pupils.

Operating mostly within the ordinary school but continuing outside it where necessary, the resource-continuum model has many advantages. Maximal flexibility is in-built, an essential feature at a time of rapid change in education in a climate of resource shrinkage. The resource continuum involves little weighty investment in capital projects or in traditions and expectations. It is geared for fluidity. Where a resource continuum is to be operated, one might expect most or all of the 'systems' featuring in the cost-effective cascade to be considered as priorities for inclusion among the services offered.

As the Preface made clear, there is no suggestion here that the 'systems' mentioned in these pages are all-inclusive. The chapter on 'miscellaneous ideas' offers some fascinating notions — which have yet to be evaluated. If and when this occurs, these and any other novel creations could be incorporated at the schematically appropriate level in either the total cascade or the cost-effective cascade — depending on the results of the evaluation.

The need for programmes of all sorts to have self-evaluation methods designed into them from the outset cannot be over-emphasised. This applies not only to novel programmes, but also to attempts to replicate programmes known to have favourable evaluation results elsewhere, since there is no guarantee of automatic transfer of programme success between environments. Attempts at *post hoc* evaluation are akin to estimating the size of the departed horse by measuring the stable exit. It is hoped that this book will have given the imaginative reader some initial ideas on *how* to build in evaluation.

Every programme must have its objectives specified in unambiguous operational terms. The objectives for the programme set by its teachers, pupils and their parents, referring teachers and schools, headteachers, administrators, politicians and so on, will all need taking into account, with conflicts resolved and a consensus reached so far as is possible. The balance between academic, behavioural and other objectives must be agreed. Distinction between long-term and short-term gains must be made, as must distinction between 'process' objectives which facilitate operational flow, and 'product' objectives which refer to final outcomes. Clarity of expectations regarding situation-specificity of any change is also necessary — how much generalisation and transfer of programme effects should be written into programme objectives?

Having achieved some clarity about purposes, the next problem is finding a method for determining whether or not the objectives are met. At this point the desirability of specifying programme objectives in observable behavioural terms becomes very evident. If data-gathering is to rely on the self-report of the perceptions of involved individuals, whose perceptions are going to be taken into account? Are these perceptions to be tapped via questionnaire, interview or other method, bearing in mind the findings mentioned earlier concerning disparity in results between these and observational studies? But can the manpower for observational data-gathering be found, from a professional or other source? If some form of testing is to be utilised, are the validities and reliabilities of tests adequate, and do such results really relate to the complexities of reality? For those systems which require an interceding change in the behaviour of adults to produce change in the behaviour of the disruptive pupil, evaluative evidence that both of these have occurred in a causally linked manner is highly desirable. Either one without the other makes something of a mockery of the programme. Can a control group be found, and is this, or a reversal or time-series research design, politically acceptable? If not, behavioural results must be compared to spontaneous remission rates. These questions are raised to be helpful rather than to deflate enthusiasm, which may be the more likely short-term effect. Practitioners may feel that the task is too arduous and time-consuming, and that advice to incorporate evaluation is impractical. However, it can certainly be argued that, on the contrary, this advice is very practical, since a degree of extra evaluative effort at an early stage can prevent the squandering of vast amounts of human and material resources subsequently.

While some of the older-established and more expensive systems have not come out of this evaluative review very well, it is certainly not the intention of this book to create new 'fashions' or set fresh bandwagons rolling. There is no suggestion here of universal 'cures'. What will work for one child will not necessarily work for another, and likewise what works in one geographical or organisational context may not in another. Nor is there any proposal that evaluative research evidence should be the only consideration in decision-making about programme establishment, since administrative, political and possibly even moral considerations may also be relevant. However, it can be strongly argued that the research evidence should inform and balance these other considerations to a far greater degree than has often proved the case. On the whole, most of us would feel more comfortable if we had some assurance that decision-makers were aware of the possible (or, preferably, probable) effects of their decisions. And at the end of the day, of course, a system must be acceptable to the people who have to work it — or should you devise your system and then find people who *can* work it?

Much of the content of this book could well be construed by those employed in systems which do not emerge well from evaluative scrutiny as an attack. Facts may certainly be threatening, but to detect an 'attack' would be to subscribe to literary anthropomorphism on a grand scale. The argument has been advanced that in a time of financial claw-back, it is safer to leave resources tied up in establishments like special schools, which are construed to be less vulnerable to resource cut-backs than smaller and more flexible operations. This contention may indeed be seductive to those who are employed in special schools, but its status remains speculative, for, despite its plausibility, no evidence to support it seems readily available. Obviously, no professionals with any concern for children with special educational needs would wish to see resources diverted away from such children. But those with such concern would surely also wish those resources available to be deployed in a maximally cost-effective way, in order that children with special needs derive the greatest possible benefit therefrom. If no extra resources are forthcoming, the evaluation evidence suggests that some redistribution of existing resources will perforce be in the best interests of the children. Naturally, the retraining process for some professionals will prove long, slow and arduous, but if the political will to do something constructive and effective for children with special educational needs is there, it does not necessarily follow that resources operated flexibly in the 'main-stream' should be any more at risk of claw-back than institution-based resources. This should particularly apply if the flexible resource builds in an evaluative process and can demonstrate to its political masters that the taxpayers are getting good value for money.

While a number of professionals may still feel that building in pro-gramme evaluation is impractical in their situation, a minority of main-stream professionals may feel that even trying out one of the less familiar systems described here would prove a practical impossibility. All the systems in the cost-effective cascade have proved effective in a range of different contexts, but that doesn't necessarily guarantee success right there where you are. Teachers obviously need to consider their own professional context and decide which venture might be the most practicable, think it through carefully, and gather the support of close colleagues. Then step-wise learning principles should be applied — test-ing your new baby system out on the most disruptive child in the school first is definitely not recommended. This child has probably been dis-ruptive for a long time, and can wait a little longer until the new system has been field-tested on smaller fry, and the professionals involved have built up some practical experience and confidence. It is also worth bear-ing in mind that part of the tailoring of new 'systems' ventures to the

specific context revolves round the question of needs assessment —
there is little point in setting up an elaborate system in a school which
is already very calm and organised and has few problems with disruptive
behaviour. Equally, however, one minor innovation in a school where
the whole organisational fabric is in disarray is also likely to be doomed
to failure.

Accepting these caveats, there is a lot to be said for going ahead and
trying something out. The experience of doing something may well
prove more valuable than a clutch of committee meetings. Some of the
approaches documented can be tried out by an individual teacher or a
small group of interested colleagues. If the initiative starts small, there
is much advantage in building in some kind of evaluation, so that in the
fullness of time convincing data of effectiveness in the local context
can be displayed which may enthuse more colleagues, and so on. In a
climate of scepticism, to solicit permission to attempt a new initiative
on the basis of a fixed-period trial or 'experiment', with evaluation built
in, will test the rational superstructure of the most heavily ballasted
antagonist, since no one should have much to lose.

In the final analysis, success in creating organisational change often
depends on the effectiveness of systems of communication flow. This
is already a major problem area for many large and organisationally
complex secondary schools. In many an institution the procedures for
communication flow would benefit from critical scrutiny as a precursor
to the establishment of any innovative programme. However, there is
nothing so absurd as a meeting called to discuss communication where
no one has anything to say because there is no focus of debate. Communication is a process, not a product, and does not operate *in vacuo*.
It may be that informative evaluative input about an innovative programme in a school, by serving as a focus for debate, could throw a
revealingly oblique light on the communication systems within the
establishment. If this book's attempt to ensure ease of availability of
evaluative evidence is found to have this kind of spin-off, so much the
better.

REFERENCES

Advisory Centre for Education (1980) 'Disruptive Units – ACE Survey', *Where*, 158, 15-16

Ahlstrom, W.M. and Havighurst, R.J. (1971) *400 Losers* (San Francisco: Jossey-Bass)

Alachua County Schools (1975) *Programs for the Emotionally Disturbed: A Handbook of Guidelines and Evaluative Data on Five Instructional Models 1974-75* (Gainesville, Florida: Alachua County Schools)

Allen, G.J. *et al.* (1976) *Community Psychology and the Schools* (New Jersey: Lawrence Erlbaum (via Wiley))

Allen, T.W. (1970) 'The Evaluation of a Program of Special Classes for "Disruptive Children" in an Urban School System', *Community Mental Health*, 6, 4, 276-84

Altman, K.I. and Linton, T.E. (1971) 'Operant Conditioning in the Classroom Setting: A Review of the Research', *The Journal of Educational Research*, 64, 6, 277-86

Asselstine, J.L. (1968) 'Public School Classes for Disturbed Children', *Canadian Psychiatric Association Journal*, 13, 4, 375-81

Atkinson, G.C.E. (1975) 'The Highfield Experiment', *New Behaviour*, 10.7.75, 54-7

Ayllon, T.A. and Roberts, M.D. (1974) 'Eliminating Discipline Problems by Strengthening Academic Performance', *J. App. Behav. Anal.*, 7, 71-6

Azrin, N.H. and Holz, W.C. (1966) 'Punishment' in W.K. Honig (ed.), *Operant Behaviour: Areas of Research and Application* (New York: Appleton-Century-Crofts)

Bailey, R.E. and Kackley, J.C. (1976) *Positive Alternatives to Student Suspension* (Clearwater, Fla.: Pinellas County District School Board)

Balbernie, R.W. (1966) *Residential Work with Children* (Oxford: Pergamon)

Bandura, E. *et al.* (1963) 'Vicarious Reinforcement and Imitative Learning', *J. Abnorm. Soc. Psychol.*, 67, 600-7

Barclay, J. (1967) 'Effecting Behaviour Change in the Elementary Classroom', *Journal of Counselling Psychology*, 14, 240-7

Barclay, J. (1970) 'Evaluating Behaviour Changes in School Psychologists', *Psychology in the Schools*, 7, 4, 320-4

Bartlett, E.F. (1970) 'Survey of Day Units for the Maladjusted Child' (unpublished Dip. Sp. Ed. Thesis: University College, Swansea)

Baxter, B. (1976) 'Tackling the Disruptive Pupil' in C. Jones-Davies and R.G. Cave (eds.), *The Disruptive Pupil in the Secondary School* (London: Ward Lock)

Bayliss, S. (1981) 'Disruptive Units: Race Study', *Times Educational Supplement*, 2.1.81

Bayliss, S. (1982) 'Rise in Suspensions for Playground Fights', *Times Educational Supplement*, 15.10.82

Baymur, F.B. and Patterson, C.H. (1960) 'A Comparison of Three Methods of Assisting Underachieving High School Students', *J. Counselling Psychol.*, 7, 2, 83-9

Becker, R.A. (1980) 'Units for Disruptive Children', personal communication

Becker, W.C. *et al.* (1967) 'The Contingent Use of Teacher Attention and Praise in Reducing Classroom Behaviour Problems', *Journal of Special Education*, 1, 287-307

Berger, M. and Wigley, V. (1980) 'Intervening in the Classroom', *Contact* (ILEA), 9, 14, 4-5

Berryman, J. *et al.* (1980) 'The Claremont Tutorial Centre' (personal communication)

Bird, C. *et al.* (1980) *Disaffected Pupils* (Uxbridge, Middlesex: Brunel University)

Birmingham Education Committee (1976) 'Provision for Disruptive Pupils', unpublished report

Bolstad, O.D. and Johnson, S.M. (1972) 'Self-regulation in the Modification of Disruptive Behaviour', *J. App. Behav. Anal.*, 5, 443-54

Bostow, D. and Bailey, J. (1969) 'Modification of Severe Disruptive and Aggressive Behaviour Using Brief Time-out and Reinforcement Procedures', *J. App. Behav. Anal.*, 2, 31-7

Bower, E.M. (1972) 'K.I.S.S. and Kids: A Mandate for Prevention', *Am. J. Orthopsychiat.*, 42, 4, 556-65

Boxall, M. (1973) 'Nurture Groups', *Concern*, 12

Breyer, N.L. *et al.* (1971) 'Behaviour Consulting from a Distance', *Psychology in the Schools*, 8, 2, 172-6

British Psychological Society (1980) *Report of a Working Party on Corporal Punishment in Schools* (Leicester: BPS)

Broden, M. *et al.* (1970a) 'Effects of Teacher Attention and a Token Reinforcement System in a Junior High School Special Education Class', *Except. Ch.*, 36, 341-9

Broden, M. *et al.* (1970b) 'Effects of Teacher Attention on Attending Behaviour of Two Boys at Adjacent Desks', *J. App. Behav. Anal.*, 3, 199-204

Broden, M. *et al.* (1971) 'The Effect of Self-recording on the Classroom Behaviour of Two Eighth-Grade Students', *J. App. Behav. Anal.*, 4, 191-9

Brown, J. *et al.* (1969) 'An Example of Psychologist Management of Teacher Reinforcement Procedures in the Elementary Classroom', *Psychology in the Schools*, 6, 336-40

Brown, T.W. (1978) 'Shaping Clear Speech in a Nine-year old Maladjusted Boy Using a Structured Procedure, Contingent Feedback and Attention', *Newsletter of the Association for Behaviour Modification with Children*, 2, 23-9

Brownsmith, K. *et al.* (1976) *Summative Evaluation: Behaviour Management Training Program* (Bloomington, Ind.: University of Indiana)

Budnick, A. and Andreacchi, J. (1967) 'Day Schools for Disturbed Boys' in P.H. Berkowitz and E.P. Rothman (eds.) *Public Education for Disturbed Children in New York City* (Springfield, Illinois: Thomas)

Burchard, J.O. and Barrera, F. (1972) 'An Analysis of Timeout and Responsive Cost in a Programmed Environment', *J. App. Behav. Anal.*, 5, 271-82

Burland, J.R. (1979) 'Behaviour Modification in a Residential School for Junior Maladjusted Boys', *Journal of the Association of Workers with Maladjusted Children*, 7, 65-79

Burland, R. *et al.* (1978) 'Strategies for Reintegrating Maladjusted Children into an Ordinary School', *Journal of the Association of Educational Psychologists*, 4, 7, 20-7

Burn, M. (1964) *Mr Lyward's Answer* (London: Hamish Hamilton)

Burns, R.B. (1978) 'The Relative Effectiveness of Various Incentives and Deterrents as Judged by Pupils and Teachers', *Educational Studies*, 4, 3, 229-43

Cally, E. and Rees, V. (1980) 'A School Unit – Its Nature and Function' in G. Upton and A. Gobell, *Behaviour Problems in the Comprehensive School* (Cardiff: Faculty of Education, University College, Cardiff)

Cantrell, R.P. and Cantrell, M.L. (1977) 'Evaluation of a Heuristic Approach to Solving Children's Problems', *Peabody Journal of Education*, 54, 3, 168-73

Carnine, D. *et al.* (1968) 'The Effects of Direct and Vicarious Reinforcement on the Behaviour of Problem Boys in an Elementary School Classroom' (unpublished manuscript: University of Illinois)

Carroll, H.M.C. (1972) 'The Remedial Teaching of Reading: An Evaluation', *Remedial Education*, 7, 1, 10-15

Chalk, J. (1975) 'Sanctuary Units in Primary Schools', *Special Education: Forward Trends*, 2, 4, 18-20

Chandler, M.J. (1973) 'Egocentrism and Anti-Social Behaviour: The Assessment and Training of Social Perspective-Taking Skills', *Developmental Psychology*, 9, 3, 326-32

Chard, P.H. (1980) 'The Individual Studies Department, Whitecross School', personal communication

Chazan, M. (1967) 'The Effects of Remedial Teaching in Reading: A Review of Research', *Remedial Education*, 2, 1, 4-12

Chazan, M. (1973) 'Special Education for Maladjusted Children and Adolescents in Norway', *J. Child Psychol. Psychiat.*, 14, 57-69

Christy, P.R. (1975) 'Does Use of Tangible Rewards with Individual Children Affect Peer Observers?', *J. App. Behav. Anal.*, 8, 187-96

Church, R.M. (1963) 'The Varied Effects of Punishment on Behaviour', *Psychol. Rev.*, 70, 369-402

Clarizio, H.F. (1968) 'Stability of Deviant Behaviour Through Time', *Mental Hygiene*, 52, 288-93

Clarizio, H.F. (1976) *Towards Positive Classroom Discipline*, 2nd edn. (New York: Wiley)

Clarizio, H.F. and Yelon, S.L. (1967) 'Learning Theory Approaches to Classroom Management', *The Journal of Special Education*, 1, 3, 267-74

Clark, B.S. (1965) 'The Acquisition and Extinction of Peer Imitation in Children', *Psychonomic Science*, 2, 147-8

Clegg, A.B. (1962) *Delinquency and Discipline* (Council and Education Press)

Coates, G.W.A. (1977) *The Effects of Disruptive Behaviour in Schools* (Leeds: CCDU, University of Leeds)

Cohen, H. (1963) 'The Academic-Activity Program at Hawthorne', *Except. Ch.*, 30, 74-9

Cohen, H.L. *et al.* (1971) 'P.I.C.A. (Programming Interpersonal Curricula for Adolescents)', paper presented at APA workshop, Washington D.C.

Cook, E. *et al.* (1972) 'A Study of Exemplary Programs for Emotionally Disturbed Children', reported in Graf, M.H. (1979)

Cook, J. (1980) 'School Based Adjustment Groups', *Journal of the Association of Educational Psychologists*, 5, 4 (part 2), 16-17

Cook, J. *et al.* (1979) *An Evaluation of the Effectiveness of Within-School Classes for Emotionally Disturbed Children* (Chichester: West Sussex Psychological Service)

Cooke, T.P. and Apolloni, T. (1976) 'Developing Positive Social-Emotional Behaviours: A Study of Training and Generalisation Effects', *J. App. Behav. Anal.*, 9, 65-78

Cooling, M. (1974) 'Educational Provisions for Maladjusted Children in Boarding Schools' (unpublished MEd Thesis: University of Birmingham)

Cooper, M.L. *et al.* (1970) 'The Experimental Modification of Teacher Attending Behaviour', *J. App. Behav. Anal.*, 3, 153-7

Coulby, D. (1980) *Division 5 Schools Support Unit: Progress Report* (London: ILEA)

Coulby, D. and Harper, T. (1981) *D.O.5 Schools Support Unit. Evaluation: Phase I* (London: ILEA)

Coulby, D. and Harper, T. (1983) *D.O.5 Schools Support Unit. Evaluation: Phase II* (London: ILEA)

Cowen, E.L. (1968) 'Effectiveness of Secondary Prevention Programs Using Non-professionals in the School Setting', *Proceedings of the 76th Annual Convention of the American Psychological Association*, 2, 705-6

Cowen, E.L. (1974) 'Geometric Expansion of Helping Services', *Journal of School Psychology*, 12, 4, 288-95

Cowen, E.L. *et al.* (1966) 'A College Student Volunteer Programme in the Elementary School Setting', *Community Mental Health Journal*, 2, 319-28

Cowen, E.L. *et al.* (1968) 'Utilization of Retired People as Mental Health Aides with Children', *Am. J. Orthopsychiat.*, 38, 900-9

Cowen, E.L. *et al.* (1969) 'Evaluation of a College Student Volunteer Program with Primary Graders Experiencing School Adjustment Problems', *Psychology in the Schools*, 6, 371-5

Cowen, E.L. *et al.* (1972) 'Follow-up Study of Maladapting School Children Seen by Non-professionals', *J. Consult. and Clin. Psychol.*, 39, 2, 235-8

Critchley, C. (1969) 'An Experimental Study of Maladjusted Children' (unpublished MA Thesis: University of Liverpool)

Csapo, M. (1972) 'Peer Models Reverse the "One Bad Apple Spoils the Barrel" Theory', *Teaching Exceptional Children*, 5, 20-4

Curtis, M. and Gilmore, C. (1981) 'Group Counselling in Secondary Schools', *Journal of the Association of Educational Psychologists*, 5, 6, 47-52

Cutler, R.L. and McNeil, E.B. (1966) *Mental Health Consultation in Schools: A Research Analysis* (Ann Arbor, Michigan: University of Michigan Dept. of Psychology)

D'Angelo, R.Y. and Walsh, J.F. (1967) 'An Evaluation of Various Therapy Approaches with Lower Socioeconomic Group Children', *Journal of Psychology*, 67, 59-64

Davie, R. *et al.* (1972) *From Birth to Seven* (London: Longman)

Davies, B. and Thorne, M. (1977) 'What Pupils Think', *Times Educational Supplement*, 23.12.77

Dawson, R.L. (1980) *Special Provision for Disturbed Pupils: A Survey* (London: Macmillan)

Deem, M.A. and Porter, W.R. (1965) *Development of a Program for the Reeducation and Rehabilitation of Emotionally Handicapped Male Adolescents within a Public School Setting* (Rockville, Maryland: Montgomery County Public Schools)

Department of Education and Science (1972) *Aspects of Special Education: Education Survey 17* (London: HMSO)

Department of Education and Science (1978a) *Truancy and Behavioural Problems in Some Urban Schools* (London: DES)

Department of Education and Science (1978b) *Behavioural Units: A Survey of Special Units for Pupils with Behavioural Problems* (London: DES)

Department of Education and Science (1980) *Educational Provision by the Inner London Education Authority* (London: DES)

Dering, A. (1980) 'Manchester Scheme for the Alleviation of Disruption in Schools' (unpublished paper: Manchester LEA)

De Roche, E.F. and Modlinski, J.J. (1977) 'Commando Academy: From Clashes to Classrooms', *Educational Leadership*, 34, 6, 429-32

District of Columbia Public Schools (1975) *Morse Crisis Intervention Centre – Project Advance. Final Report* (Washington, DC: DC Public Schools)

Docking, J.W. (1980) *Control and Discipline in Schools* (London: Harper & Row)

Drabman, R.S. and Spitalnik, R. (1973) 'Social Isolation as a Punishment Procedure: A Controlled Study', *Journal of Experimental Child Psychology*, 16, 236-49

Drabman, R.S. *et al.* (1973) 'Teaching Self-Control to Disruptive Children', *J. Abnorm. Psychol.*, 82, 1, 10-16

Duke, D.L. (ed.) (1979) *Classroom Management (Part II)* (Chicago: University of Chicago Press for the National Society for the Study of Education)

Dupont, H. (1975) 'Concluding Comments' in H. Dupont (ed.), *Educating Emotionally Disturbed Children*, 2nd edn. (New York: Holt, Rinehart & Winston)

D'Zurilla, T.J. and Goldfried, M.R. (1971) 'Problem Solving and Behaviour Modification', *J. Abnorm. Psychol.*, 8, 107-26

Eisenberg, L. (1969) 'Child Psychiatry: the Past Quarter-century', *Am. J. Orthopsychiat.*, 39, 3, 389-401

Evans, M. *et al.* (eds.) (1970) *Day Schools for Maladjusted Children* (Hertford: Association of Workers for Maladjusted Children)

Eysenck, H.J. (1960) 'The Effects of Psychotherapy' in H.J. Eysenck (ed.), *Handbook of Abnormal Psychology* (London: Pitman)

Felixbrod, J.J. and O'Leary, D.K. (1973) 'Effects of Reinforcement on Children's Academic Behaviour as a Function of Self-Determined and Externally Imposed Contingencies', *J. App. Behav. Anal.*, 6, 241-50

Filipczak, J. *et al.* (1979) 'Issues in Multivariate Assessment of a Large-scale Behaviour Program', *J. App. Behav. Anal.*, 12, 593-613

Fischer, J. (1978) 'Does Anything Work?', *Journal of Social Service Research*, 1, 3, 215-43

Fiske, E.B. (1977) 'Schools Developing Alternatives to Student Suspensions', *New York Times*, 18.5.77

Fo, W.S.O. and O'Donnell, C.R. (1974) 'The Buddy System: Relationship and Contingency Conditions in a Community Intervention Program for Youth, etc.', *J. Consult. Clin. Psychol.*, 42, 163-9

Forehand, R. and MacDonough, T.S. (1975) 'Response Contingent Outcome: An Examination of Outcome Data', *Eur. J. Behav. Anal. Modif.*, 1, 109-15

Foulkes, M. (1980) 'Special Units and Classes for Children with Behaviour Problems', personal communication

Francis, M. (1979) 'Disruptive Pupils: Labelling a New Generation', *New Approaches in Multi-Racial Education*, 8, 1, 6-9

Francis, M. (1980a) '"Sin Bins": Narrow and Racist or Working Well?', *Times Educational Supplement*, 5.12.80, p. 13

Francis, M. (1980b) 'Disruptive Units – Labelling a New Generation', *Where*, 158, 12-14

Friedlander, F. (1968) 'A Comparative Study of Consulting Processes and Group Development', *J. App. Behav. Sci.*, 4, 377-99

Fry, L. *et al.* (1980) 'Behaviour Modification at Lea Green School', *Journal of the Association for Behaviour Modification with Children*, 4, 1

Gallagher, P.A. (1972) 'Structuring Academic Tasks for Emotionally Disturbed Boys', *Exceptional Children*, 38, 9

Galloway, D.M. (1976) 'Size of School, Socio-economic Hardship, Suspension Rate and Persistent Unjustified Absence from School', *Brit. J. Educ. Psychol.*, 46, 1, 40-7

Galloway, D.M. (1979) 'A Study of Persistent Absence from School in Sheffield: Prevalence and Associated Educational, Psychological and Social Factors' (unpublished PhD Thesis: Sheffield City Polytechnic)

Galloway, D.M. (1980) 'Special Groups for Disturbing Pupils in Ordinary Secondary Schools', *Sheffield Education Research: Current Highlights*, 2, 9-10

Galloway, D.M. (1981) 'Sheffield School and Home Project', *Journal of the Association of Educational Psychologists*, 5, 6, 39-47

Galloway, D.M. and Goodwin, C. (1979) *Educating Slow-learning and Maladjusted Children* (London: Longman)

Galloway, D.M. *et al.* (1978) 'Absence from School and Behaviour Problems in School', *Therapeutic Education*, 6, 2, 28-34

Galloway, D.M. *et al.* (1982) *Schools and Disruptive Pupils* (London: Longman)

Garibaldi, A.M. (ed.) (1979) *In-school Alternatives to Suspension: Conference Report* (Washington DC: Dept. Health, Education and Welfare for National Institute of Education)

Geshuri, Y. (1972) 'Observational Learning: Effects of Observed Reward and Response Patterns', *J. Educ. Psychol.*, 63, 374-80

Giebink, J.W. *et al.* (1968) 'Teaching Adaptive Responses to Frustration to Emotionally Disturbed Boys', *J. Consult. Clin. Psychol.*, 32, 3, 366-8

Glavin, J.P. (1968) 'Spontaneous Improvement in Emotionally Disturbed Children' (unpublished PhD dissertation: Diss. Abs., 28, 3503A)

Glavin, J.P. (1972) 'Persistence of Behaviour Disorders in Children', *Except. Ch.*, 38, 5

Glavin, J.P. (1973) 'Follow-up Behavioural Research in Resource Rooms', *Except. Ch.*, 40, 211-13

Glavin, J.P. (1974) 'Behaviourally Oriented Resource Rooms: A Follow-up', *Journal of Special Education*, 8, 337-47

Glavin, J.P. and Quay, H.C. (1969) 'Behaviour Disorders', *Review of Educational Research*, 39, 1, 83-102

Glavin, J.P. *et al.* (1971a) 'Behavioural and Academic Gains of Conduct Problem Children in Different Classroom Settings', *Except. Ch.*, 37, 441-6

Glavin, J.P. *et al.* (1971b) 'An Experimental Resource Room for Behaviour Problem Children', *Except. Ch.*, 38, 131-7

Gloss, G.G. (1968) *Experimental Programs for Emotionally Handicapped Children in Ohio* (Columbus, Ohio: Divn. of Special Education, Ohio State Dept. of Education)

Glynn, E.L. (1970) 'Classroom Applications of Self-determined Reinforcement', *J. App. Behav. Anal.*, 3, 2, 123-32

Gnagey, W. (1975) *The Psychology of Discipline in the Classroom* (New York: Macmillan)

Goldstein, A.P. *et al.* (1980) *Skill-streaming the Adolescent* (Champaign, Ill.: Research Press)

Goodman, G. (1972) *Companionship Therapy* (San Francisco: Jossey-Bass)

Goodwin, D.L. (1966) 'Training Teachers in Reinforcement Techniques to Increase Pupil Task-Oriented Behaviour: An Experimental Evaluation', *Diss. Abstr. Int.*, 27, 674-A

Graf, M.H. (1979) 'A Study of a Public School Program for the Severely Emotionally Disturbed' (unpublished D Ed Thesis: University of Illinois, Urbana-Champaign)

Graubard, P.S. (1969a) 'Teaching Strategies and Techniques for the Education of Disruptive Groups and Individuals' in P.S. Graubard (ed.), *Children Against Schools* (Chicago: Follett Educational)

Graubard, P.S. (1969b) 'Utilizing the Group in Teaching Disturbed Delinquents to Learn', *Except. Ch.*, 36, 267-72

Great Falls Public Schools (1971) *Behaviour Modification of Emotionally Disturbed Youth: Final Report of Educational Adjustment Classes* (Montana: Great Falls Public Schools)

Griffiths, D. (1980) 'The Special Education Team', personal communication

Griffiths, D. *et al.* (1981) 'A Team Approach to Disruption', *Special Education: Forward Trends*, 8, 1, 8-10

Grunsell, R. (1979) 'Suspensions and the Sin-Bin Room: Soft Option for Schools', *Where*, 153, 307-9

Hall, R.V. *et al.* (1968a) 'Instructing Beginning Teachers in Reinforcement Procedures which Improve Classroom Control', *J. App. Behav. Anal.*, 1, 315-22

Hall, R.V. *et al.* (1968b) 'Effects of Teacher Attention on Study Behaviour', *J. App. Behav. Anal.*, 1, 1-12

Hall, R.V. *et al.* (1970) 'Teachers and Parents as Researchers Using Multiple Baseline Designs', *J. App. Behav. Anal.*, 3, 4, 247-55

Hall, R.V. *et al.* (1971) 'The Effective Use of Punishment to Modify Behaviour in the Classroom', *Educational Technology*, 2, 4, 24-6

Hamill, D. and Wiederholt, J.L. (1972) *The Resource Room: Rationale and Implementation* (Pennsylvania: Journal of Special Education Press)

Haring, N.G. and Phillips, E.L. (1962) *Educating Emotionally Disturbed Children* (New York: McGraw-Hill)

Haring, N.G. and Whelan, R.J. (1965) 'Experimental Methods in Education and Management of Emotionally Disturbed Children' in N.J. Long *et al.* (eds.), *Conflict in the Classroom* (Belmont, Calif.: Wadsworth)

Harris, V.W. and Sherman, J.A. (1973) 'Use and Analysis of the "Good Behaviour Game" to Reduce Disruptive Classroom Behaviour', *J. App. Behav. Anal.*, 6, 3, 405-17

Harrison, B. (1980) 'Peripatetic Provision for Disruptive Pupils', personal communication

Harrop, A. (1978) 'Behaviour Modification in the Ordinary School Setting', *Journal of the Association of Educational Psychologists*, 4, 7, 3-15

Haughton, E. (1968) 'Training Counsellors as Advisers of Precision Teaching', paper presented at CEC Convention, New York

Haussmann, S.E. (1979) 'De-institutionalisation of Status Offenders: an In-school Suspension Project', paper presented at Annual International Convention, Council for Exceptional Children

Hawkins, P.J. (1974) 'Training Teachers in Classroom Management', *Behaviour Modification Newsletter*, 5, 7-14

Hawkins, R. *et al.* (1967) 'Results of Operant Conditioning Techniques in Modifying the Behaviour of Emotionally Disturbed Children', paper presented at Annual International Council for Exceptional Children, St Louis

Hedderly, R. (1978) 'Orange Juice Therapy', *Journal of the Association of Educational Psychologists*, 4, 9, 24-8

Hedderly, R. (1981) 'Class Size and Achievement in School', *Journal of the Association of Educational Psychologists*, 5, 5, 45-7

Henry, S.E. and Killman, P.R. (1979) 'Student Counselling Groups in Senior High School Settings: An Evaluation of Outcome', *Journal of School Psychology*, 17, 1, 27-46

Heron, T.E. (1978) 'Punishment: A Review of the Literature with Implications for the Teacher of Mainstreamed Children', *Journal of Special Education*, 12, 3, 243-52

Hewett, F.M. (1968) *The Emotionally Disturbed Child in the Classroom* (Boston: Allyn & Bacon)

Hewett, F.M. *et al.* (1969) 'The Santa Monica Project: Evaluation of an Engineered Classroom Design with Emotionally Disturbed Children', *Except. Ch.*, 35, 523-9

Hewett, F.M. and Blake, P.R. (1973) 'Teaching the Emotionally Disturbed' in R.M.W. Travers (ed.), *Second Handbook of Research on Teaching* (Chicago: Rand-McNally)

Highfield, M.E. and Pinsent, A. (1972) *A Survey of Rewards and Punishments in School* (London: Newnes (for NFER))

Hirshoren, A. and Heller, G.G. (1979) 'Programs for Adolescents with Behaviour Disorders: the State of the Art', *Journal of Special Education*, 13, 3, 275-81

Hobbs, S.A. and Forehand, R. (1977) 'Important Parameters in the Use of Timeout with Children: A Re-examination', *J. Behav. Ther. and Exp. Psychiat.*, 8, 365-70

Hulbert, C.M. *et al.* (1977) 'A Teacher-Aide Programme in Action', *Special Education: Forward Trends*, 4, 1, 27-31

Human Resources Research Organisation (1974) *Comprehensive Services for Children: Third Year Evaluation Report* (Dothan, Alabama: HUMRRO)

Hunter, W.F. and Ratcliffe, A.W. (1968) 'The Range Mental Health Centre: Evaluation of a Mental Health Programme', *Community Mental Health Journal*, 4, 3, 260-7

ILEA (1978a) *Survey of Corporal Punishment in I.L.E.A. Secondary Schools* (London: ILEA)

ILEA (1978b) 'Disruptive Pupils Programme: Individual Schemes Where the Annual Cost Exceeds £25,000', *Report of the Chief Education Officer to the Schools Sub-Committee, 17.10.78.* (Ref. ILEA 8573/5) (London: ILEA)

ILEA (1978c) 'Disruptive Pupils Programme', *Report of the Chief Education Officer to the Schools Sub-Committee, 17.11.78.* (Ref. ILEA 8640/10) (London: ILEA)

ILEA (1979a) 'Disruptive Pupils Programme', *Report of the Chief Education Officer to the Schools and Staff Sub-Committees, 18.4.79.* (Ref. ILEA 9215/5) (London: ILEA)

ILEA (1979b) 'Procedures for School Support Centres', *Report of the Chief Education Officer to the Schools Sub-Committee, 18.4.79.* (Ref. ILEA 9214/5) (London: ILEA)

ILEA (1980a) *Support Centres Programme Monitoring Study: First Annual Report* (RS 744/80) (London: ILEA Research and Statistics Division)

ILEA (1980b) 'Disruptive Pupils', *Report of the Chief Education Officer to the Schools Sub-Committee, 26.1.78.* (Appendix to Education Committee Agenda of 7.3.78) (London: ILEA)

ILEA (1981a) *Ethnic Census of School Support Centres and Educational Guidance Centres* (RS 784/81) (London: ILEA Research and Statistics Division)

ILEA (1981b) *Support Centres Programme – Monitoring and Evaluation Report No. 2 RS 788/81* (London: ILEA Research and Statistics Division)

Illera, J. (1977) 'A Model Program for Disturbed Adolescents in a Day Facility', conference paper, Convention of Council for Exceptional Children, Atlanta, Georgia

Ingram, P. (1972) 'I.L.E.A. Tackle Their Aggressive Pupils', *Times Educational Supplement*, 3.3.72, no. 2963, p. 6

Irving, J.E. (1975) 'Friends Unlimited: Adolescents as Helping Resources', *Children Today*, 4, 4, 14-17

Iscoe, I. *et al.* (1967) 'Some Strategies in Mental Health Consultation' in E.L. Cowen *et al.* (eds.), *Emergent Approaches to Mental Health Problems* (New York: Appleton-Century-Crofts)

Jeffrey, C.R. and Jeffrey, J.A. (1969) 'Dropouts and Delinquents: An Experimental Program in Behaviour Change', *Education and Urban Society*, 1, 325-36

Jenkins, J.R. and Mayhall, W.F. (1976) 'Development and Evaluation of a Resource Teacher Program', *Except. Ch.*, 43, 21-9

Jesinkey, W.J. and Stern, J.R. (1974) *Lost Children: a Descriptive Study of the Systems for the Education of Emotionally Handicapped Children in the City of New York* (New York: Alternative Solutions for Exceptional Children Inc)

Johnson, C.A. and Katz, J. (1973) 'Using Parents as Change Agents for their Children: A Review', *J. Ch. Psychol. Psychiat.*, 14, 181-200

Kauffmann, J.M. *et al.* (1977) 'Follow-up in Classroom Behaviour Modification: Survey and Discussion', *Journal of School Psychology*, 15, 343-48

Kaufman, K.F. and O'Leary, K.D. (1972) 'Reward, Cost and Self-evaluation Procedures for Disruptive Adolescents in a Psychiatric Hospital School', *J. App. Behav. Anal.*, 5, 293-309

Kazdin, A. (1973) 'The Effect of Vicarious Reinforcement on Attentive Behaviour in the Classroom', *J. App. Behav. Anal.*, 6, 71-8

Kazdin, A. and Klock, J. (1973) 'The Effect of Non-verbal Teacher Approval on Student Attentive Behaviour', *J. App. Behav. Anal.*, 6, 643-54

Kendall, P.C. *et al.* (1975) 'Timeout Duration and Contrast Effects: A Systematic Evaluation of a Successive Treatments Design', *Behaviour Therapy*, 6, 609-15

Kirby, F.D. and Toler, H.C. (1970) 'Modification of Pre-School Isolate Behaviour', *J. App. Behav. Anal.*, 3, 309-14

Klein, G. *et al.* (eds.) (1967) *COVERT (Children Offered Vital Educational Retraining and Training)* (Tucson, Arizona: Tucson Public Schools)

Koenig, C.H. (1967) 'Precision Teaching with Emotionally Disturbed Pupils', *Research Paper No. 17* (Children's Rehabilitation Unit, University of Kansas)

Kolvin, I. *et al.* (1976) 'Maladjusted Pupils in Ordinary Schools', *Special Education: Forward Trends*, 3, 3, 15-19

Kolvin, I. *et al.* (1981) *Help Starts Here: the Maladjusted Child in the Ordinary School* (London: Tavistock)

Kounin, J.S. (1970) *Discipline and Group Management in Classrooms* (New York: Holt, Rinehart & Winston)

Krumboltz, J.D. and Goodwin, D.L. (1966) *Increasing Task-oriented Behaviour: An Experimental Evaluation of Training Teachers in Reinforcement Techniques* (Final Report, University of Stanford School of Education)

Kvaraceus, W.C. and Ulrich, W.E. (1959) *Delinquent Behaviour: Principles and Practices* (Washington, DC: National Educational Association of the US)

Labon, D. (1974) 'Some Effects of School-Based Therapy', *Journal of the Association of Educational Psychologists*, 3, 28-34

Lane, D.A. (1978) *The Impossible Child*, vol. 2 (London: ILEA)

Lane, D.A. (1983) *Whatever Happened to the Impossible Child?*, vol. 3 (London: Islington EGC, ILEA)

Lane, D.A. and Millar, R.R. (1977) 'Dealing with Behaviour Problems in School: a New Development', *Community Health*, 8, 155-9

Lansdown, R. (1971) 'School-based Care', *Journal of the Association of Educational Psychologists*, 2, 9, 22-3

Lawrence, J. *et al.* (1981) *Dialogue on Disruptive Behaviour* (Croydon, Surrey: P.J.D. Press)

Leach, D.J. and Raybould, E.C. (1977) *Learning and Behaviour Difficulties in School* (London: Open Books)

Leeds City Council (1975) 'Interim Report of the Committee on the Problem of Disruptive Children' (unpublished document, Department of Education, Leeds)

Lemkau, P.V. and Pasamanick, B. (1957) 'Problems in Evaluation of Mental Health Programs', *Amer. J. Orthopsychiat.*, 27, 55

Levitt, E.E. (1957) 'The Results of Psychotherapy with Children: an Evaluation', *J. Consult. Psychol.*, 21, 189-96

Levitt, E.E. (1963) 'Psychotherapy with Children: a Further Evaluation', *Behav. Res. Ther.*, 1, 45-51

Levitt, E.E. *et al.* (1959) 'A Follow-up Evaluation of Cases Treated at a Community Child Guidance Clinic', *Amer. J. Orthopsychiat.*, 29, 337-49

Lewis, M.D. (1970a) 'The Effects of Counselling and Consultation, etc.', *Elementary School Guidance Counselling*, 5, 1, 44-52

Lewis, M.D. (1970b) 'Elementary School Counselling and Consultation: Their Effects on Teachers' Perceptions', *The School Counsellor*, 18, 1, 49-52

Lewis, W. (1965) 'Continuity and Intervention in Emotional Disturbance', *Except. Ch.*, 31, 465-75

Lisle, J.D. (1968) 'The Comparative Effectiveness of Various Group Procedures Used with Elementary Pupils with Personal-Social Adjustment Problems', *Diss. Abstr. Int.*, 28, 11, 448-A

Liverpool Education Committee (1974) *The Suspended Child: Teachers Advisory Committee Report* (Liverpool: Liverpool Education Committee)

Long, B.E. (1970) 'A Model for Elementary School Behavioural Science as an Agent of Primary Prevention', *Amer. Psychol.*, 25, 371-4

Long, B.E. (1974) 'Increasing Depth of Self-Perception in Children Through a Course in Psychology', *Counselling and Values*, 18, 2, 117-22

Long, J. and Madsen, C.H. (1975) 'Five-year Olds as Behavioural Engineers for Younger Students in a Day-Care Centre' in E. Ramp and G. Simb (eds.), *Behaviour Analysis: Areas of Research and Application* (Englewood Cliffs, New Jersey: Prentice-Hall)

Longworth-Dames, S.M. (1977) 'The Relationship of Personality and Behaviour to School Exclusion', *Educational Review*, 29, 3, 163-77

Lovitt, T.C. (1973) 'Self-Management Projects with Children with Behaviour Disabilities', *Journal of Learning Disabilities*, 6, 138-50

Lovitt, T.C. and Curtiss, K.A. (1969) 'Academic Response Rate as a Function of Teacher and Self-imposed Contingencies', *J. App. Behav. Anal.*, 2, 49-53

Lovitt, T.C. *et al.* (1973) 'The Deceleration of Inappropriate Comments by a Natural Consequence', *Journal of School Psychology*, 11, 149-56

Lunzer, E.A. (1960) 'Aggressive and Withdrawing Children in the Normal School — Patterns of Behaviour', *Brit. J. Educ. Psychol.*, 30, 1-10

McAllister, L.W. *et al.* (1969) 'The Application of Operant Conditioning Techniques in a Secondary School Classroom', *J. App. Behav. Anal.*, 2, 4, 277-85

McCaffrey, I. and Cumming, J. (1967) *Behaviour Patterns Associated with Persistent Emotional Disturbances of School Children in Regular Classes of Elementary Grades* (Onondaga, New York State: Mental Health Research Unit, Dept. of Mental Hygiene)

McCullough, J.P. (1972) 'An Investigation of the Effects of Model Group Size Upon Response Facilitation in the High School Classroom', *Behav. Ther.*, 3, 561-6

McDonald, W.S. *et al.* (1970) 'Contingency Counselling by School Personnel: an Economical Model of Intervention', *J. App. Behav. Anal.*, 3, 3, 175-82

McKenzie, H.S. *et al.* (1968) 'Behaviour Modification of Children with Learning Disabilities using Grades as Tokens and Allowances as Back-up Reinforcers', *Except. Ch.*, 34, 745-53

McKeown, D. (1975) 'Generalisation to the Classroom of Principles of Behaviour Modification Taught to Teachers', *Behav. Res. and Ther.*, 13, 85-92

McKinnon, A.J. (1970) 'Parent and Pupil Perceptions of Special Classes for Emotionally Disturbed Children', *Except. Ch.*, 37, 4

McLaughlin, T.F. (1976) 'Self-control in the Classroom', *Rev. Educ. Res.*, 46, 631-63

McLaughlin, T.F. and Malaby, J.E. (1975) 'Elementary Schoolchildren as Behavioural Engineers' in E. Ramp and G. Simb (eds.), *Behaviour Analysis: Areas of Research and Application* (Englewood Cliffs, New Jersey: Prentice-Hall)

McNamara, E. (1979) 'The Use of Self-recording in Behaviour Modification in a Secondary School', *Behav. Psychother.*, 7, 3, 57-66

McNamara, E. and Harrop, L.A. (1979) 'Behaviour Modification in the Secondary School: A Cautionary Tale', *Occasional Papers of the Division of Educational and Child Psychology, British Psychological Society*, 3, 2, 38-41

McNamara, E. and Heard, C. (1976) 'Self-control through Self-recording', *Special Education: Forward Trends*, 3, 2, 21-3

McNamara, E. and Moore, B. (1978) 'Special Educational Treatment for Maladjusted Pupils in a Day Centre', *Journal of the Association of Educational Psychologists*, 4, 7, 15-20

McWilliams, S.S. and Finkel, N.J. (1973) 'High School Students as Mental Health Aides in the Elementary School Setting', *J. Consult. Clin. Psychol.*, 40, 39-42

Macmillan, A. and Kolvin, I. (1977) 'Behaviour Modification in Teaching Strategy', *Educational Research*, 20, 1, 10-21

Macmillan, D.L. *et al.* (1973) 'The Role of Punishment in the Classroom', *Except. Ch.*, 40, 85-96

Macmillan, D.L. and Morrison, G.M. (1979) 'Educational Programming' in H.C. Quay and J.S. Werry (eds.), *Psychopathological Disorders of Childhood*, 2nd edn. (New York: Wiley)

Madsen, C.H. *et al.* (1968) 'An Analysis of the Reinforcing Function of "Sit Down" Commands' in R.K. Parke (ed.), *Readings in Educational Psychology* (Boston: Allyn & Bacon)

Madsen, C.H. and Madsen, C.K. (1973) *Teaching Discipline: Behavioural Principles Towards a Positive Approach* (Boston: Allyn & Bacon)

Main, G.C. and Munro, B.C. (1977) 'A Token Reinforcement Programme in a Public Junior High School', *J. App. Behav. Anal.*, 10, 1, 93-4

Maloney, D.M. *et al.* (1976) 'Teaching Conversation – Related Skills to Predelinquent Girls', *J. App. Behav. Anal.*, 9, 371-5

Manchester Education Committee (1974) 'Social Education Project', unpublished paper

Mannino, F.V. and Shore, M.F. (1972) 'Research in Mental Health Consultation' in S.E. Golann and C. Eisdorfer (eds.), *Handbook of Community Mental Health* (New York: Appleton-Century-Crofts)

Mannino, F.V. and Shore, M.F. (1975) 'Effecting Change Through Consultation' in Mannino, F.V. *et al.*, *The Practice of Mental Health Consultation* (Adelphi, Maryland: US Dept. of Health, Education and Welfare)

Marlowe, R.H. *et al.* (1978) 'Severe Classroom Behaviour Problems: Teachers or Counsellors', *J. App. Behav. Anal.*, 11, 53-6

Marshall, M. (1971) 'The Effect of Special Educational Treatment of Maladjusted Pupils in a Day School', *Journal of the Association of Educational Psychologists*, 2, 10, 23-5

Martin, M. *et al.* (1968) 'Programming Behaviour Change and Reintegration into School Milieux of Extreme Adolescent Deviates', *Behav. Res. and Ther.*, 6, 371-83

Marzillier, J. (1978) 'Outcome Studies of Skills Training: A Review' in P. Trower *et al.* (eds.), *Social Skills and Mental Health* (London: Methuen)

Masat, L.J. *et al.* (1980) 'Transitional Strategies for Mainstreaming Emotionally Disturbed Students', paper presented at Annual International Convention of the Council for Exceptional Children, Philadelphia

Maughan, B. and Ouston, J. (1979) 'Fifteen Thousand Hours: Findings and Implications', *Trends*, 4, 18-24

Mayer, G.R. *et al.* (1968) 'The Use of Punishment in Modifying Student Behaviour', *Journal of Special Education*, 2, 323-8

Medland, M.B. and Stachnik, T.J. (1972) 'Good Behaviour Game: a Replication and Systematic Analysis', *J. App. Behav. Anal.*, 5, 1, 45-51

Meichenbaum, D. (1973) 'Cognitive Factors in Behaviour Modification: Modifying What Clients Say to Themselves' in C.M. Franks and G.T. Wilson (eds.), *Annual Review of Behaviour Therapy, Theory and Practice* (New York: Brunner/Marzel)

Meichenbaum, D. and Cameron, R. (1973) 'Stress Inoculation: A Skills Training Approach to Anxiety Management' reported in M.J. Mahoney (1974), *Cognition and Behaviour Modification* (Cambridge, Mass.: Ballinger)

Mezzano, J. (1968) 'Group Counselling with Low-motivated Male High School Students – Comparative Effects of Two Uses of Counsellor Time', *J. Educ. Res.*, 61, 5, 222-4

Mickleburgh, P.J. (1980) *Atherstone Day Unit: Fifth Annual Report* (Atherstone: Warwickshire LEA)

Milburn, C.W. (1980) 'A Positive Rewards System' in G. Upton and A. Gobell, *Behaviour Problems in the Comprehensive School* (Cardiff: Faculty of Education, University College)

Miller, R.J. *et al.* (1968) *Educational Programming in Simulated Environments for Seriously Emotionally Handicapped Junior High School Students: Final Report* (Baltimore: Maryland State Dept. of Education)

Minde, K.K. and Werry, J.S. (1968) 'The Response of School-children in a Low Socio-economic Area to Extensive Psychiatric Counselling of Their Teachers: A Controlled Evaluation', paper presented to meeting of American Psychiatric Association, Boston

Minkin, N. *et al.* (1976) 'The Social Validation and Training of Conversational Skills', *J. App. Behav. Anal.*, 9, 127-39

Minuchin, S. *et al.* (1967) 'A Project to Teach Learning Skills to Disturbed Delinquent Children', *Am. J. Orthopsychiat.*, 37, 3, 558-67

Mitchell, S. and Shepherd, M. (1966) 'A Comparative Study of Children's Behaviour at Home and at School', *Brit. J. Educ. Psychol.*, 36, 248-54

Morgan, L. (1980) personal communication

Morse, W.C. (1965) 'The Crisis Teacher' in N.J. Long *et al.* (eds.), *Conflict in the Classroom* (Belmont, Calif.: Wadsworth)

Morse, W.C. (1966) 'Public Schools and the Disturbed Child' in P. Knoblock (ed.), *Intervention Approaches in Educating Emotionally Disturbed Children* (Syracuse, New York: Syracuse University Press)

Morse, W.C. *et al.* (1964) *Public School Classes for the Emotionally Handicapped: A Research Analysis* (Washington, DC: Council for Exceptional Children)

Mortimore, P. *et al.* (1983) *Behaviour Problems in Schools: An Evaluation of Support Centres* (Beckenham: Croom Helm)

Moseley, D. (1975) *Special Provision for Reading* (Slough: NFER)

Munro, N. (1981) 'Belt Ban Has Not Led to Worse Classroom Behaviour', *Times Educational Supplement*, 9.10.81

Musgrave, P.W. (1977) 'Corporal Punishment in Some English Elementary Schools: 1900-1939', *Research in Education*, 17, 1-11

National Association of Secondary School Principals (1976) 'Disruptive Behaviour: Prevention and Control', *The Practitioner*, 2, 2, 1-12

Nelson, C.M. *et al.* (1973) 'Behaviourally Disordered Peers as Contingency Managers', *Behaviour Therapy*, 4, 270-6

Nelson, C.M. and Kauffman, J.M. (1977) 'Educational Programming for Secondary School Age Delinquent and Maladjusted Pupils', *Behavioural Disorders*, 2, 2, 102-13

Nelson, R. (1979) in A.M. Garibaldi (ed.) *In-School Alternatives to Suspension: Conference Report* (Washington DC: Dept. Health, Education and Welfare for National Institute of Education)

Nietzel, M.T. *et al.* (1977) *Behavioural Approaches to Community Psychology* (London: Pergamon Press)

North Carolina State Dept. of Public Instruction (1977) *Emotionally Handicapped Pupils: Developing Appropriate Educational Programs* (Raleigh: NCSDPI)

O'Hagan, F.J. and Edmunds, G. (1983) 'Pupils' Attitudes Towards Teachers' Strategies for Controlling Disruptive Behaviour', *British Journal of Educational Psychology* (in press)

Ohio State Dept. of Education (1974) *Utilising Volunteers for Children with*

Behavioural Disabilities (Columbus, Ohio: Division of Special Education, Ohio State D. of E.)

Ojemann, R.H. (1967) 'Incorporating Psychological Concepts in the School Curriculum', *Journal of School Psychology*, 5, 195-204

O'Leary, K.D. (1978) 'The Operant and Social Psychology of Token Systems' in A.C. Catania and T.A. Brigham (eds.), *Handbook of Applied Behaviour Analysis* (New York: Halstead Press)

O'Leary, K.D. and Drabman, R. (1971) 'Token Reinforcement Programs in the Classroom: A Review', *Psychol. Bull.*, 75, 6, 379-98

O'Leary, K.D. *et al.* (1970) 'The Effects of Loud and Soft Reprimands on the Behaviour of Disruptive Students', *Except. Ch.*, 36, 145-55

O'Leary, S.G. and O'Leary, K.D. (1976) 'Behaviour Modification in the School' in H. Leitenberg (ed.), *Handbook of Behaviour Modification* (Englewood Cliffs, NJ: Prentice-Hall)

Olsen, T. (1974) 'Alternative Educational Programs', *J. of Reading*, 18, 190-1

Onondaga County School Boards Association (1964) *Persistence of Emotional Disturbances reported among Second and Fourth Grade Children* (Syracuse, New York: Mental Health Research Unit)

Page, D.P. and Edwards, R.P. (1978) 'Behaviour Change Strategies for Reducing Disruptive Classroom Behaviour', *Psychology in the Schools*, 15, 3, 413-18

Parke, R.D. (1969) 'Effectiveness of Punishment as an Interaction of Intensity, Timing, Agent Nurturance, and Cognitive Structuring', *Child Development*, 40, 1, 213-35

Patterson, G.R. (1974) 'Intervention for Boys with Conduct Problems: Multiple Settings, Treatments and Criteria', *J. Consult. Clin. Psychol.*, 42, 471-80

Pearl, S. (1979) 'The Responsibility Resource Rooms and Resource Centre, etc.', *Behavioural Disorders*, 4, 3, 163-7

Pease, G.A. and Tyler, V.O. (1979) 'Self-regulation of Timeout Duration in the Modification of Disruptive Classroom Behaviour', *Psychology in the Schools*, 16, 1, 101-5

Petrie, I.R.J. (1962) 'Residential Treatment of Maladjusted Children: a Study of Some Factors Related to Progress in Adjustment', *Brit. J. Educ. Psychol.*, 32, 29-37

Phillips, E.L. and Haring, N.G. (1959) 'Results from Special Techniques for Teaching Emotionally Disturbed Children', *Except. Ch.*, 26, 64-7

Pierce-Jones, J. *et al.* (1968) *Child Behaviour Consultation in Elementary Schools, etc.* (Austin, Texas: University of Texas Press)

Plummer, S.E. (1977) 'Functional Considerations in the Use of Time-out from a Schedule of Positive Reinforcement: A Basic and Applied Analysis', *Diss. Abstr. Int.*, 37, 8-B, 4194-5

Presland, J.L. (1973) 'Helpers for Disturbing Children', *Journal of the Association of Educational Psychologists*, 3, 4, 36-9

Presland, J.L. (1980) 'Behaviour Modification and Secondary Schools' in G. Upton and A. Gobell (eds.), *Behaviour Problems in the Comprehensive School* (Cardiff: Faculty of Education, University College)

Presland, J.L. (1981) 'Modifying Behaviour Long-term and Sideways', *Journal of the Association of Educational Psychologists*, 5, 6, 27-30

Quay, H.C. (1973) 'Special Education: Assumptions, Techniques and Evaluative Criteria', *Except. Ch.*, 40, 165-70

Quay, H.C. *et al.* (1972) 'The Modification of Problem Behaviour and Academic Achievement in a Resource Room', *J. Sch. Psychol.*, 10, 2, 187-97

Quay, H.C. and Glavin, J.P. (1970) *The Education of Behaviourally Disordered Children in the Public School Setting: Interim Report* (Philadelphia: Temple University)

Rabinowitz, A. (1975) 'Sanctuaries', unpublished paper

Rachman, S. (1971) *The Effects of Psychotherapy* (London: Pergamon)

Rawlinson, G. (1980) 'Disruptive Units', personal communication

Reger, R. and Koppman, M. (1971) 'The Child-oriented Resource Room', *Except. Ch.*, 37, 460-2

Reinert, H.R. (1980) *Children in Conflict*, 2nd edn. (St Louis: C.V. Mosby)

Rendell, B. (1980) 'The Individual Studies Department, Whitecross School, Lydney, Glos.' in G. Upton and A. Gobell (eds.), *Behaviour Problems in the Comprehensive School* (Cardiff: Faculty of Education, University College, Cardiff)

Reynolds, D. and Murgatroyd, D.S. (1977) 'The Sociology of Schooling and the Absent Pupil: the School as a Factor in the Generation of Truancy' in H.C.M. Carroll (ed.), *Absenteeism in South Wales* (Swansea: Faculty of Education, University College)

Richmond, C.A. (1978) 'Practical Application of a Behaviour Modification Management System Project', paper presented at Annual International Convention, Council for Exceptional Children, Kansas City

Rideout, E. (1980) 'Pencoed Comprehensive School Support Class', unpublished document

Rinn, R.C. (1975) 'Training Parents of Behaviourally Disordered Children in Groups: A Three-Year Program Evaluation', *Behav. Ther.*, 6, 378-87

Robertson, J. (1981) *Effective Classroom Control* (London: Hodder and Stoughton)

Robin, A. (1976) 'The Turtle Technique: An Extended Case Study of Self-control in the Classroom', *Psychology in the Schools*, 13, 4

Robins, L.N. (1973) 'Evaluation of Psychiatric Services for Children in the U.S.' in J.K. Wing and H. Hafner (eds.), *Roots of Evaluation* (London: Oxford University Press)

Roe, M.C. (1965) *Survey into Progress of Maladjusted Pupils* (London: ILEA)

Rogers, C. (1980) 'Disruptive Children', personal communication

Rose, R. (1978) 'The Effect of the Use of Behaviour Modification Techniques on the Social and Academic Performance of Maladjusted Boys' (unpublished BSc Report: University of Bradford)

Rosenfeld, G.W. (1972) 'Some Effects of Reinforcement on Achievement and Behaviour in a Regular Classroom', *Journal of Educational Psychology*, 63, 3, 189-93

Rotter, J.B. (1966) 'Generalised Expectancies for Internal versus External Control of Reinforcement', *Psychol. Monog.*, 80, 1

Rubin, E.Z. *et al.* (1966) *Emotionally Handicapped Children and the Elementary School* (Detroit: Wayne State University Press)

Rutter, M. and Graham, P. (1966) 'Psychiatric Disorder in 10 and 11 year old Children', *Proceedings of the Royal Society of Medicine*, 59, 382-7

Rutter, M. *et al.* (1979) *Fifteen Thousand Hours: Secondary Schools and Their Effects on Children* (London: Open Books)

Sachs, D.A. (1973) 'Efficacy of Time-out Procedures in a Variety of Behaviour Problems', *J. Behav. Ther. and Exp. Psychiat.*, 4, 237-42

Sallows, J.O. (1972) 'Responsiveness of Deviant and Normal Children to Naturally Occurring Consequences', *Diss. Abstr. Int.*, 6092-B, 226

Sarason, I.G. and Sarason, B.R. (1974) *Constructive Classroom Behaviour* (New York: Behavioural Publications)

Schmidt, G.W. and Ulrich, R.E. (1969) 'Effects of Group Contingent Events on Classroom Noise', *J. App. Behav. Anal.*, 2, 171-9

Schowengerdt, R.V. *et al.* (1976) 'An Examination of Some Bases of Teacher Satisfaction with School Psychological Services', *Psychology in the Schools*, 13, 3, 269-75

Schultz, E.W. *et al.* (1971) 'Special Education for the Emotionally Disturbed', *Except. Ch.*, 38, 4

Schumaker, J.B. *et al.* (1977) 'An Analysis of Daily Report Cards and Parent-Managed Privileges in the Improvement of Adolescents' Classroom Performance', *J. App. Behav. Anal.*, 10, 3, 449-64

Shaw, O. (1965) *Maladjusted Boys* (London: Allen & Unwin)

Shepherd, M. *et al.* (1966) 'Childhood Behaviour Disorders and the Child Guidance Clinic: an Epidemiological Study', *J. Child. Psychol. Psychiat.*, 3, 39-52

Shepherd, M. *et al.* (1971) *Childhood Behaviour and Mental Health* (London: University of London Press)

Sherman, J.A. and Bushell, D. (1974) 'Behaviour Modification as an Educational Technique' in F.D. Horowitz (ed.), *Review of Child Development Research*, vol. 4 (Chicago: University of Chicago Press)

Shields, R. (1962) *A Cure of Delinquents* (London: Heinemann)

Shores, R.E. and Hambrich, P.A. (1969) 'Effect of Cubicles in Educating Emotionally Disturbed Children', *Except. Ch.*, 36, 21-4

Siegel, L.J. and Steinman, W.M. (1975) 'The Modification of a Peer-observer's Classroom Behaviour as a Function of his Serving as a Reinforcing Agent' in E. Ramp and G. Simb (eds.), *Behaviour Analysis: Areas of Research and Application* (Englewood Cliffs, New Jersey: Prentice-Hall)

Simmonds, E. (1965) 'Testing Results in the Day Maladjusted School', *Educational Review*, 17, 144-50

Sindelar, P.T. and Deno, S.L. (1978) 'The Effectiveness of Resource Programming', *Journal of Special Education*, 12, 17-28

Skinski, E.J. *et al.* (1978) '3R Program: Responsibility, Re-education and Reality', paper presented at World Congress on Future Special Education, Stirling

Smith, D.C. (1969) *A Community Helper Program for Children with Behaviour and Learning Disorders* (Columbus, Ohio: Ohio State University)

Smith, D.H. (ed.) (1973) *Disruptive Students* (Albany, New York: Bureau of School Social Services, New York State Education Dept)

Smith, M. (1980) 'Disruptive Children', personal communication

Society of Teachers Opposed to Physical Punishment (1979) *Reading List* (Croydon: STOPP)

Solomon, R.L. (1964) 'Punishment', *Amer. Psychol.*, 19, 239-53

Solomon, R.W. and Wahler, R.G. (1973) 'Peer Reinforcement Control of Classroom Problem Behaviour', *J. App. Behav. Anal.*, 6, 49-56

Spaulding, R.L. and Showers, B. (1974) 'Applications of the Spaulding System of Classroom Behavioural Analysis in Field Settings', paper presented at Annual Meeting of American Educational Research Association, Chicago

Spivack, G. and Shure, M.B. (1974) *Social Adjustment of Young Children: A Cognitive Approach to Solving Real Life Problems* (San Francisco: Jossey-Bass)

Sprinthall, N.A. (1974) 'A Cognitive Developmental Curriculum – the Adolescent as Psychologist', *Counselling and Values*, 18, 2, 94-101

Stein, E.M. *et al.* (1976) 'A Contingency Management Day Program for Adolescents Excluded from Public School', *Psychology in the Schools*, 13, 2, 185-91

Stern, C. *et al.* (1971) *Therapeutic Interventions with Emotionally Disturbed Preschool Children* (Los Angeles: University College of LA)

Stokes, T.F. and Baer, D.M. (1977) 'An Implicit Technology of Generalisation', *J. App. Behav. Anal.*, 10, 349-67

Strain, P.S. *et al.* (1976) 'The Role of Peers in Modifying Classmates' Social Behaviour: A Review', *Journal of Special Education*, 10, 351-6

Stratford, R.J. and Cameron, R.J. (1979) 'Aiming at Larger Targets, *Occasional Papers of the Division of Educational and Child Psychology, British Psychological Society*, 3, 2, 47-62

Surratt, P.R. *et al.* (1969) 'An Elementary Student as a Behavioural Engineer', *J. App. Behav. Anal.*, 2, 85-92

Swailes, A. (1979) 'Experiment at Parkhead Centre', *Special Education: Forward Trends*, 6, 1, 23-5

Sweeney-Rader, J. *et al.* (1980) 'School Suspensions: An In-House Prevention Model', *Children Today*, 9, 2, 19-21

Tattum, D.P. (1982) *Disruptive Pupils in Schools and Units* (Chichester: Wiley)

Tennessee State Department of Mental Health (1975) *A Prevention-Intervention Model for Students' Learning and Behaviour Problems: Final Report 1974-75* (TSDMH, Nashville)

Tharp, R.G. and Wetzel, R.J. (1969) *Behaviour Modification in the Natural Environment* (New York: Academic Press)

Thomas, D.R. *et al.* (1968) 'Production and Elimination of Disruptive Classroom Behaviour by Systematically Varying Teachers' Behaviour', *J. App. Behav. Anal.*, 1, 33-45

Times Educational Supplement (1981) 'Disco Plan to Beat Disruptive Behaviour', *TES*, 1.5.81 (referring to J. Lawrence *et al.*, 1981)

Times Educational Supplement (1982) 'Separate Development' (feature), *TES*, 9.7.82, 17-19

Tobiessen, J. and Shai, A. (1971) 'A Comparison of Individual and Group Mental Health Consultation with Teachers', *Community Mental Health Journal*, 7, 3, 218-26

Topping, K.J. (1976) *Bibliography: Special Units and Classes for Children with Behaviour Problems*, Research Paper No. 7 (Halifax: Calderdale Psychological Service)

Topping, K.J. (1977a) 'An Evaluation of the Long-term Effects of Remedial Teaching', *Remedial Education*, 12, 2, 84-6

Topping, K.J. (1977b) *Evaluation of Psychological Services and Mental Health Consultation: A Bibliography* (Halifax: Calderdale Psychological Service)

Topping, K.J. (1978) 'Consumer Confusion and Professional Conflict in Educational Psychology', *Bull. Br. Psychol. Soc.*, 31, 265-7

Topping, K.J. and Quelch, T. (1976) *Special Units and Classes for Children with Behaviour Problems – An Informal Survey of L.E.A. Practice*, Research Paper No. 6 (Halifax: Calderdale Psychological Service)

Truax, C.B. and Carkhuff, R.R. (1967) *Towards Effective Counselling and Psychotherapy* (Chicago: Aldine)

Tuckey, L. *et al.* (1973) *Handicapped School Leavers* (Windsor: NFER)

Tyler, M.M. (1971) 'A Study of Some Selected Parameters of School Psychologist/ Teacher Consultation' (unpublished PhD Thesis, University of Kansas: Diss. Abstr. Int. 321,0, 5626-A)

Tyler, V. and Brown, G. (1967) 'The Use of Swift Brief Isolation as a Group Control Device for Institutionalised Delinquents', *Behav. Res. & Ther.*, 5, 1-9

Upshur, B. (date not known), *Analysis of Satellite Program for Disruptive Children. Final Report* (Washington, DC: National Institute of Education) (ED 136468, EC 093188)

Vacc, N.A. (1968) 'A Study of Emotionally Disturbed Children in Regular and Special Classes', *Except. Ch.*, 35, 3

Vacc, N.A. (1972) 'Long Term Effects of Special Class Intervention for Emotionally Disturbed Children', *Except. Ch.*, 39, 1

Wahler, R.G. and Erickson, M. (1969) 'Child Behaviour Therapy: a Community Program in Appalachia', *Behav. Res. Ther.*, 7, 1, 71-8

Walker, H. *et al.* (1968) 'Special Class Placement as a Treatment Alternative for Deviant Behaviour in Children' in F. Benson (ed.), *Modifying Deviant Social Behaviours in Various Classroom Settings* (Eugene, Oregon: University of

Oregon), also as: Walker, H.M. *et al.* (1969) *Special Class Placement as a Treatment Alternative for Deviant Behaviour in Children* (Monograph No. 1.) (Eugene, Oregon: Dept. Special Education, University of Oregon)

Walker, H.M. and Buckley, N.K. (1972) 'Programming Generalisation and Maintenance of Treatment Effects Across Time and Settings', *J. App. Behav. Anal.*, 5, 209-24

Walker, H.M. and Hops, H. (1973) 'The Use of Group and Individual Reinforcement Contingencies in the Modification of Social Withdrawal' in L.A. Hammerlynch *et al.* (eds.), *Behaviour Change: Methodology, Concepts and Practice* (Champaign, Illinois: Research Press)

Walters, R.H. *et al.* (1965) 'Timing of Punishment and Observation of Consequences to Others as Determinants of Response Inhibition', *J. Exp. Ch. Psychol.*, 2, 10-30

Ward, B.A. and Tikunoff, W.J. (1979) 'Utilising Nonteachers in the Instructional Process' in D.L. Duke (ed.), *Classroom Management: The 78th Yearbook of the National Society for the Study of Education*, Part II (Chicago: University of Chicago Press for NSSE)

Warner, S.P. *et al.* (1979) 'Relative Effectiveness of Teacher Attention and the "Good Behaviour Game" in Modifying Disruptive Classroom Behaviour', *J. App. Behav. Anal.*, 10, 4, 737-44

Warnock, H.M. (1978) *Report of the Committee of Enquiry into the Education of Handicapped Children and Young People* (London: HMSO)

Webb, A.B. and Cormier, W.H. (1972) 'Improving Classroom Behaviour and Achievement', *Journal of Experimental Education*, 41, 92-6

Webster, R.E. (1976) 'A Time-out Procedure in a Public School Setting', *Psychology in the Schools*, 13, 1, 72-6

Weinstein, L. (1969) 'Project Re-Ed Schools for Emotionally Disturbed Children: Effectiveness as Viewed by Referring Agencies, Parents and Teachers', *Except. Ch.*, 35, 9, 703-11

Werner, J. *et al.* (1975) 'Intervention Package: An Analysis to Prepare Juvenile Delinquents for Encounters with Police Officers', *Criminal Justice and Behaviour*, 2, 55-84

Westmacott, E.V.S. (1980) 'Disruptive Children', personal communication

Wheldall, K. and Austin, R. (1980) 'Successful Behaviour Modification in the Secondary School', *Occasional Papers of the Division of Educational and Child Psychology, British Psychological Society*, 4, 3, 3-9

White, G.D. *et al.* (1972) 'Timeout Duration and the Suppression of Deviant Behaviour in Children', *J. App. Behav. Anal.*, 5, 111-120

White, M.A. (1979) 'Considerations in the Integration of Behaviourally Disordered Students into the Regular Classroom', paper presented at Annual International Convention of the Council for Exceptional Children, Dallas

White-Blackburn, G. *et al.* (1977) 'The Effects of a Good Behaviour Contract on the Classroom Behaviour of Sixth-Grade Students', *J. App. Behav. Anal.*, 10, 2, 312-20

Whitley, A.D. (1971) 'Counsellor-teacher Consultations including Video Analysis to Reduce Undesirable Student Responses', *Diss. Abstr. Int.*, 32, 4, 2413-B

Wildman, R.W. and Wildman, R.W. (1975) 'The Generalisation of Behaviour Modification Procedures: A Review, with Special Emphasis on Classroom Applications', *Psychology in the Schools*, 12, 432-8

Williams, J. (1979) 'In-School Alternatives to Suspension: Why Bother?' in A.M. Garibaldi (ed.), *In-School Alternatives to Suspension: Conference Report* (Washington DC: US National Institute of Education)

Williams, N. (1961) 'Criteria of Recovery of Maladjusted Children in Residential School' (unpublished MA Thesis: University of Durham)

Wright, D. (1973) 'The Punishment of Children' in B. Turner (ed.), *Discipline in Schools* (London: Ward Lock)

Wright, H.J. and Payne, T.A.N. (1979) *An Evaluation of a School Psychological Service* (Winchester: Hampshire Education Dept)

York, R. *et al.* (1972) 'Exclusion from School', *J. Child Psychol. Psychiat.*, 13, 259-66

Zax, M. *et al.* (1966) 'A Teacher-aide Program for Preventing Emotional Disturbances in Young Schoolchildren', *Mental Hygiene*, 50, 406-15

Bibliography of Unused Items

(A list of items which were not drawn upon for one or more of the reasons detailed in the Preface.)

Ayllon, T. *et al.* (1972) 'Disruptive Behaviour and Reinforcement of Academic Performance', *Psychological Record*, 22, 315-23

Bardon, J.I. *et al.* (1976) 'Psychosituational Classroom Intervention: Rationale and Description', *Journal of School Psychology*, 14, 2, 97-104

Berger, A. and Mitchell, G. (1978) 'Multitude of Sin-Bins', *Times Educational Supplement*, 7.7.78

Bird, C. *et al.* (1980) *Disaffected Pupils* (Uxbridge: Educational Studies Unit, Brunel University)

Bowman, P.H. (1959) 'Effects of a Revised School Program on Potential Delinquents', *Annals of the American Academy of Political and Social Science*, 322, 53-61

Braaten, S. (1979) 'The Madison School Program: Programming for Secondary Level Severely Emotionally Disturbed Youth', *Behavioural Disorders*, 4, 3, 153-62

Central Regional Council Education Dept. (1980) *Child Guidance Service Report 1977-79* (Stirling: Central Regional Council Education Dept)

Central Regional Working Party (1978) *Truancy and Indiscipline in Schools in Scotland* (Stirling: Central Regional Council)

Cope, C. and Anderson, E. (1977) *Special Units in Ordinary Schools* (Windsor: NFER)

Dain, P. (1977) 'Disruptive Children and the Key Centre', *Remedial Education*, 12, 4, 163-7

Dee, V.D. (1972) 'Contingency Management in a Crisis Class', *Except. Ch.*, 38, 8, 631-4

Dickinson, D. (1974) 'But What Happens When You Take That Reinforcement Away?', *Psychology in the Schools*, 11, 158-60

Evans, M. *et al.* (1978) 'Schools Council Project: The Education of Disturbed Pupils in England and Wales', *Journal of the Association of Workers with Maladjusted Children*, 6, 1, 17-26

Gallagher, P.A. (1972) 'Structuring Academic Tasks for Emotionally Disturbed Boys', *Except. Ch.*, 38, 9

Gardner, J.E. (1975) *Paraprofessional Work with Troubled Children* (New York: Gardner Press (via J. Wiley))

Gartner, A. *et al.* (1979) *Educational Services for Students with Special Needs* (New York: Center for Advanced Study in Education, City University)

Graubard, P.S. (1969) *Children Against Schools: The Education of Disturbed and Delinquent Children* (Chicago: Follett Educational Corp)

Heal, K. (1978) 'Misbehaviour Among School Children: The Role of the School in Strategies for Prevention', *Policy and Politics*, 6, 321-32

Hewett, F.M. (1967) 'Educational Engineering with Emotionally Disturbed Children', *Except. Ch.*, 33, 459-67

Hobbs, N. (1966) 'Helping Disturbed Children', *Amer. Psychol.*, 21, 1105-15

Hoghughi, M. (1978) *Troubled and Troublesome* (London: Burentt Books)

Hulbert, C.M. *et al.* (1977) 'A Teacher-Aide Programme in Action', *Special Education: Forward Trends*, 4, 1, 27-31

Hunkin, J. and Alhadeff, G. (1976) 'The Hermitage Adjustment Unit, Ilfracombe School', *Therapeutic Education*, 6, 1, 13-18

Jeffrey, L.I.H. *et al.* (1979) 'Generic Training in the Psychological Management of Children and Adolescents', *Journal of the Association of Workers with Maladjusted Children*, 7, 1, 32-43

Jones, N.J. and Davies, D. (1975) 'Special Adjustment Units in Comprehensive Schools', *Therapeutic Education*, 3, 1, 43-9

Jones-Davies, C. and Cane, R.G. (eds.) (1976) *The Disruptive Pupil in the Secondary School* (London: Ward Lock)

Knoblock, P. (1963) 'Critical Factors Influencing Educational Programming for Disturbed Children', *Except. Ch.*, 30, 124-9

Knoblock, P. (ed.) (1966a) *Educational Programming for Emotionally Disturbed Children* (Syracuse, New York: Syracuse University Press)

Knoblock, P. (ed.) (1966b) *Intervention Approaches in Educating Emotionally Disturbed Children* (Syracuse, New York: Syracuse University Press)

Kolvin, I. *et al.* (1975) 'Action Research in Child Psychiatry' in A.F. Laing (ed.), *Trends in the Education of Children with Special Learning Needs* (Swansea: Faculty of Education, University College of Swansea)

Kounin, J.S. *et al.* (1966) 'Managing Emotionally Disturbed Children in Regular Classrooms', *J. Educ. Psychol.*, 57, 1, 1-13

Kounin, J.S. and Obradovic, S. (1968) 'Managing Emotionally Disturbed Children in Regular Classrooms: A Replication and Extension', *Journal of Special Education*, 2, 2, 129-35

Kvaraceus, W.C. (1962) 'Helping the Socially Inadapted Pupil in the Large City Schools', *Except. Ch.*, 28, 399-404

Lane, D.A. (1978) *The Impossible Child*, vol. 1 (London: ILEA)

Lansdown, R.G. (1975) 'Day Schools and Units for Maladjusted Children' in A.F. Laing (ed.), *Trends in the Education of Children with Special Learning Needs* (Swansea: Faculty of Education, University of Swansea)

Lazerson, D.B. (1978) '"I Must Be Good If I can Teach" – Peer Tutoring with Aggressive and Withdrawn Children', paper presented at World Congress on Future Special Education, Stirling

Love, H.D. (1972) *Educating Exceptional Children in Regular Classrooms* (Springfield, Illinois: Charles C. Thomas)

Lowenstein, L.F. (1975) *Violent and Disruptive Behaviour in Schools* (Hemel Hempstead: National Association of Schoolmasters)

Macy, D.J. *et al.* (1979) *In Retrospect: 1977-78 Special Education Research* (Dallas: Texas Dept. of Research and Evaluation)

Minuchin, S. *et al.* (1967) 'A Project to Teach Learning Skills to Disturbed, Delinquent Children', *Amer. J. Orthopsychiat.*, 37, 3, 558-67

Morse, W. (1977) 'The Psychology of Mainstreaming Socio-emotionally Disturbed Children' in A. Pappanikou and J. Paul (eds.), *Mainstreaming Emotionally Disturbed Children* (Syracuse, New York: Syracuse University Press)

National Union of Teachers (1966) *Discipline in Schools* (London: NUT)

O'Hagan, F. (1980) 'Special Units Now and Beyond', *Special Education: Forward Trends*, 7, 3, 8-10

Pellman, R. *et al.* (1977) 'The Van: A Mobile Approach to Services for Adolescents', *Social Casework*, 58, 5, 268-75

Presland, J. (1972) 'Helping the Maladjusted Child', *Journal of the Association of Educational Psychologists*, 3, 2, 31-40

Quay, H.C. *et al.* (1966) 'Remediation of the Conduct Problem Child in the Special Class Setting', *Except. Ch.*, 32, 509-15

Ramp, E. (1971) 'Delayed Time-out as a Procedure for Reducing Disruptive Classroom Behaviour: A Case Study', *J. App. Behav. Anal.*, 4, 235-9

Rhodes, W.C. (1963) 'Curriculum and Disordered Behaviour', *Except. Ch.*, 30, 61-6

Robbins, R.C. *et al.* (1967) 'The School as a Selecting-Labelling System', *J. Sch. Psychol.*, 5, 4, 270-9

Rubin, R. and Balow, B. (1971) 'Learning and Behaviour Disorders: A Longitudinal Study', *Except. Ch.*, 38, 293-9

Safford, A.L. and Watts, C.A. (1967) 'An Evaluation of a Public School Program for Emotionally Handicapped Children', *California Journal of Educational Research*, 18, 125-32

Saunders, B.T. (1971) 'The Effect of the Emotionally Disturbed Child in the Public School Classroom', *Psychology in the Schools*, 8, 23-6

Scheuer, A.L. (1971) 'The Relationship Between Personal Attributes and Effectiveness in Teachers of the Emotionally Disturbed', *Except. Ch.*, 37, 723-31

Schworm, R.W. (1976) 'Models in Special Education: Considerations and Cautions', *Journal of Special Education*, 10, 2, 179-86

Seely, T. *et al.* (1974) *Behavior Disorders Program Design* (Douglasville, Georgia: Douglas County School System)

Shannon, F.J. (ed.) (1979) *Specialised Learning Provision for Alienated Children in the Secondary School (Conference Report)* (Glasgow: Notre Dame College of Education)

Snapp, M. *et al.* (1973) 'Development of In-school Psychoeducational Services for Emotionally Disturbed Children', *Psychology in the Schools*, 10, 4, 392-6

Spencer, D. (1980) 'Disruptive Units "being misused"', *Times Educational Supplement*, 5.12.80, p. 5

Thacker, J. (1980) 'Teaching Interpersonal Problem Solving Skills to Maladjusted Children', *Journal of the Association of Educational Psychologists*, 5, 4 (part 2), p. 23

Turner, B. (ed.) (1973) *Discipline in Schools* (London: Ward Lock)

Vacc, N.A. and Kirst, N. (1977) 'Emotionally Disturbed Children and Regular Classroom Teachers', *Elementary School Journal*, 77, 4, 309-17

Weaver, A.F. (1968) 'A Survey of the Treatment of Maladjusted Children within the Educational System in England' (unpublished PhD thesis: Oxford University)

Wilson, M.D. *et al.* (1978) 'Disturbed Children in Special Schools', *Special Education: Forward Trends*, 4, 2, 8-10

Wilson, M. and Evans, M. (1980) *Education of Disturbed Pupils* (London: Methuen)

Wolstenholme, F. *et al.* (1976) 'Promoting Mental Health in School', *Special Education: Forward Trends*, 3, 4, 15-18

Bibliography of Items Unlocatable in the UK

Cook, E. *et al.* (1972) *A Study of Exemplary Programs for Emotionally Disturbed Children* (New York: General Learning Corporation)

Drevlow, R. (1975) 'Pupil Personnel Workers and SLBP Students', *Pupil Personnel Services* (Minnesota Dept. of Education), 4, 2, 41-5

Lane, D.A. (1977) 'Aspects of the Use of Behaviour Modification in Secondary Schools', *Bull. Bri. Assoc. Behav. Psychother.*, 5, 76-9

Long, N. and Morse, W.C. (1965) 'Special Classes for Children with Social and Emotional Problems in Public School' in W. Wattenberg (ed.), *Social Maladjustment* (Chicago: National Society for the Study of Education)

McKinnon, A.J. (1969) 'A Follow-up and Analysis of the Effects of Placement in Classes for Emotionally Disturbed Children in Elementary School' (unpublished PhD thesis: University of Michigan)

INDEX